W9-DIM-083

Only
a President ...

Only
a President ...

American Management Association, Inc.

Standard Book Number: 8144–5189–6

Library of Congress catalog card number: 75–80869

First Printing

Contributors

William M. Allen
Robert O. Barber
Berkley W. Bedell
S. Clark Beise
Bert S. Cross
Lewis B. Cullman
W. E. Danner
George S. Dively
David R. Fairbairn
Clarence Francis
Robert W. Galvin
Abraham Goodman
Crawford H. Greenewalt
Earl F. Harris
John W. Joanis
Frederick R. Kappel
Louis B. Lundborg
Harold M. Marko

Alfred J. Marrow
William H. McElwain
Rudolph A. Peterson
Edward A. Ring
W. F. Rockwell, Jr.
John W. Rollins
Fortune Peter Ryan
David Sarnoff
Henry Schindall
H. H. Scott
Charles E. Spahr
Robert C. Townsend
Lyndall F. Urwick
W. E. Uzzell
Lawrence P. White
Elmer L. Winter
Charles E. Zimmerman

Contents

8

Only
a President ...

Introducing . . . The President

THERE are many ways to run a company successfully. Similarly, there are many ways to conduct the president's job successfully—and many kinds of people can do it. All presidents, however, must contend with the very special set of circumstances and problems that go with the job of chief executive officer. They cannot be evaded. They must be met head-on. And it is these problems that make the presidential post, in comparison with all other executive assignments, so different, so difficult, and so challenging.

The differences are both in kind and in degree. No responsibility in the organization is of the same kind as the president's. His is the *final* responsibility for what happens. He cannot share it. It belongs to his job, and his alone.

No matter how high other executives rank in the company, they carry only a part of the total responsibility. Nor do they have even the *final* responsibility for their part; for in the end the president alone is accountable for total results. "If something goes seriously wrong," says one chief

13

executive, "the most expendable man in the company is the president. That's the way it is, and that's the way it should be."

The president's job must by its nature be a lonely one. He is at the apex of the organizational pyramid. This position of eminence separates him from every other executive in the company—a separation that gives rise to a number of problems.

The president must exercise restraint in talking with other company officers. The executives who report to him are under no such strictures. They can discuss their problems freely with one another, ask who is making progress in the department or division and who is making trouble, exchange ideas on who are possible successors and what their strengths and weaknesses may be. They can talk over and compare notes on a thousand and one other matters— in short, go through the free and easy communication process that, in human relations particularly, allows a man to think out loud, to learn from others, and to shake down opinions into firm conclusions.

In contrast, the president must be extremely careful about what he says in these areas, and in the one where such talk is most helpful—that of people and personalities —he must avoid discussion altogether when it might involve members of his management team. The chief executive who discusses an officer of his company with another officer asks for trouble and disruption. His only recourse is to go outside the management group.

The job of president is so full of contradictions that it

has been called "impossible." It clearly is not—too many men are doing first-class work in the chief executive's chair for that to be true. Nevertheless, the problems of the presidency are enough to frighten off all but the stout-hearted, or perhaps the naïve.

For example: The complexity of the president's job makes delegation of major responsibilities a "must." Only the extraordinary man can get away with applying a "do it yourself" concept to the work. Yet delegation of important tasks by the president takes a special kind of courage going far beyond that needed by the executive on a lower level.

When delegation by a division or department head goes wrong, the blow is cushioned. The total welfare of the company is rarely at stake, and the chief executive officer is always there as a backstop for support, guidance, and perhaps consolation. But, when the president delegates, it usually involves a vital segment of the business and failure can be extremely costly.

Hence, the president had better be sure that the man to whom he delegates can carry out the assignment. Yet, in such a matter, who can really be sure? And, when the president's personal responsibility is so all-embracing, doesn't it seem folly to delegate at all? But delegate he must, since the presidential job cannot be carried (except by a handful of supermen) without doing so.

Another contradiction involves the president's appraisal of his own performance. How well is he doing, and what can he do to improve his effectiveness? It is extremely important for the president to come as close as possible to the exact truth, for nothing less than the success or failure of the company may be at stake. Nevertheless, it's all but impossible for him to obtain the candid appraisal he needs from people within the company itself, who are often in the best position to give him an informed opinion. No one wants to analyze his superior's performance for him; and, even if he does, completely frank appraisals are rare.

In addition to the challenges inherent in the job, the president faces all the immediate problems that other executives must deal with, but to a more intense degree and on a larger scale and a more complex scene of action. This extends to all aspects of his work. He sets the style for his organization. What he says, what he does, and (to the extent that it is discernible) what he thinks have tremendous impact on others in the organization. He must be constantly alert to the possible effect of his actions, even though the effect may be unintended. He can seldom let down; he must always be on guard. If he looks worried, everyone who sees him worries. If he is hesitant, so will his associates hesitate. His failure to acknowledge a subordinate's smiling "Good morning" can set off emotional hurricanes at high executive levels in a man's office or in his home. A nuance in the president's voice, intentional or not, can start ripples that travel unexpected distances and have unforeseeable results.

Every executive faces the question of developing a successor. But a poor choice of successor by a department or division head is unlikely to injure a company seriously; the same mistake on the part of a president can be, and has been, ruinous. And, if the president sets up his chosen successor as a "fair-haired boy," he may well become the target of shots from his associates. Once again, the results will be much more damaging than a similar mistake in judgment would be within a division.

Another problem, common to many executive posts but intensified at the presidential level, stems from the tendency to insulate the boss from bad news. "Surprise is the enemy of good management." A vital part of the chief executive's job is knowing what's *really* going on in the organization. Breaking through the protective blanket thrown around him is a delicate and difficult matter, since it should be done in ways that avoid accusations of interference or spying. Few presidents feel that they have found wholly satisfactory answers to this problem.

The protective blanket creates another difficulty for the chief executive. "Know thyself" is a basic rule of management. Because of his great influence, the president should apply it more than anyone else. But here again his position of eminence and isolation makes it difficult. No one in his company is likely to tell him unpleasant truths about himself, though they may be precisely what he most needs to know.

To a greater degree than any other officer in the organization, the president is involved with people and their relations with one another. They are his most pressing and continuous concern. Yet, by their nature, they create the most difficult management problems to solve. They rarely lend themselves to the rational methods of solution that sales, production, research, and financial questions usually do. Few formulas or figures can help in finding answers; the era of the computer still has little to offer. The president must navigate in relatively uncharted waters, and he must navigate well or wreck the ship.

The differences in the president's work, compared to that of lower-echelon executives, extend to apportionment of time. In spite of the words in his title, the chief executive officer cannot confine himself to execution. By and large, the less time he puts on execution and the more he puts on long-range planning, policy making, and seeing that decisions in those areas are carried out, the better a chief executive officer he is likely to be.

This is not always true; in a smaller company the president may also be the top salesman, the chief money man, the production head, or the captain of the collective bargaining team. That, however, only makes the task more difficult. He still must make plans, set policies, and see that they are carried out. And, in the end, the characteristics and problems of the presidential job in the smaller company have many more similarities with, than differences from, those in the large organization.

More detailed analysis of the chief executive's work uncovers other difficulties and paradoxes. The chief executive must plan for the future. Yet he must not let planning absorb him to such an extent that today's operating results suffer. He must keep in close touch with what is going on. Yet he should not "pry" or "interfere."

The chief executive must be a management generalist.

But often he must become a specialist as well, and in fields he knows little about—as, for instance, when he probes deeply into problems, some quite technical, that seriously affect the welfare of the business as a whole.

The president must develop and maintain the kind of personal relations with people on his management team that create a climate in which, preferably, they *want* to do what he wishes. Yet he must do it without lowering himself in their eyes, or seeming to condescend, or showing special favor of any kind.

If the company is successful, the chief gives his management team the credit. If it fails, he alone takes the blame. Potentially—and sometimes actually—he is in the position of the field general who loses a battle. The reasons may be totally beyond the general's control: failure of supply, failure of diplomacy, events in areas beyond his jurisdiction. But, to the high command, the simple fact is that he has lost the battle. Therefore, he must be removed.

Finally, as the man responsible for his organization's policies and growth, the chief executive officer is not only the key man in the company. He is a key man in free enterprise as well. On the sum total of the decisions he and others at his level make largely rests the future of our social system. His decisions and actions create most of the wealth on which its material strength rests. His philosophy and conduct form a substantial part of its moral base.

He must be the innovator, the great advocate of change and progress. "Good enough" can never be good enough for him. His is a restless search for the new and the better.

The many decisions he makes to gain those ends must be in accord with a fundamental, well-thought-out philosophy of life and of society. Only through an understanding of his philosophy can those he leads, those who depend on him, know what he stands for and comport themselves accordingly.

Planner, doer, trouble shooter, burden bearer, generalist, specialist, free-enterpriser, philosopher—what individual can possibly measure up to the requisites of the president's job? And, even if such an individual existed, why would he want to take on the tremendous challenges that are constantly being thrust upon the president?

Judged by results achieved, the fact is, however, that a number of people meet the qualifications fully. Furthermore, most men who become president enjoy the position, for a variety of reasons: the sense of achievement that they derive from it, the feeling of pride and power that goes with successful leadership, the satisfaction of being in a position to exert a positive influence on society as a whole. Given the choice of living their lives over again, the overwhelming majority of chief executives would go right back where they started and follow the same careers they have pursued.

All the men represented in this book are—or have been —chief executives. Some have "graduated" from president to become board chairman; some are now retired. Certainly all know from personal experience both the problems and the rewards of being a president. And, as W. E. Uzzell says in the opening chapter from which the book's title is drawn, "only a president thinks like a president"; only a few are able to anticipate what the job will really be like and so start planning for it.

This, then, is the purpose of the book: to help prospective presidents—those whose elevation is imminent and those who privately nourish the hope, unsuspected by friends or associates, that "some day" it may just happen to them—begin thinking seriously about the top job in the organization and its implications for every ambitious executive.

Only a President
Thinks like a President

W. E. Uzzell

SEVERAL years ago when I was vice president of marketing, the company president and I had a close call in an airplane. When we landed, he turned to me and said, "I was thinking up there—what would happen to the company if we were killed?"

I distinctly remember my first thoughts in the plane. They were for my wife and family. But, now that I am president, I am sure my first thoughts also would include the company.

Many things have happened to me since that day in

W. E. UZZELL is President, Royal Crown Cola Co., Columbus, Georgia.

April 1965 when I sat down at my desk as newly elected president of Royal Crown Cola. I had the feeling that from then on my life was going to be different. I was right. A tipoff came when a company employee who had known me for years as Bill met me in the hall and called me Mr. Uzzell.

But the really important change was in the new way I thought of myself: Pride in my powerful new position quickly gave way to the realization that I was no longer ambitious for myself. I had transferred my ambition to the company and to those connected with it. Being responsible for "my people" used to mean the sales staff. Now I feel responsible for the hundreds of company employees, the stockholders, and the people across the country who bottle and sell our product.

In the first days, I also discovered that the president is constantly being watched. And with some skill he can use this fact to good advantage. One day, for example, I decided to start my office day at eight in the morning. Without a word from me, staff members who had been accustomed to arriving around nine started to report to the office an hour earlier, too. "I see you're really getting results from that new eight o'clock rule," an executive said to me. In trying to stretch my own day, I had—without premeditation—raised a work standard. I filed that lesson away for a time when I might want to set a really important example.

Getting in early became more and more important as I uncovered a growing number of problems. I began to understand why those magic decisions that are supposed to cure all corporate ills don't just come pouring out of the president's office.

My predecessor had directed the company through prosperous but turbulent years of growth. Maintaining the rapid growth pace took precedence over many other things. I was faced with the problem of bringing up to date, for example, several management development and incentive programs. They had been set aside during the hectic early years of growth.

We introduced profit sharing on a porter-to-president basis, increased fringe benefits, spelled out job descriptions and established performance standards, revaluated all positions, and adopted higher salary levels. The April 1 tradition of handing out salary increases was abolished; instead, all increases now are based on performance reviews—employees' contributions to the company. These programs gave company morale a healthy boost. Good employees, in particular, welcomed the new performance standards because they guaranteed that salaries and promotion would not be at the mercy of someone's arbitrary opinion or whim.

We told employees that we were interested in the development of their abilities. These programs proved that we meant what we said.

I was going through my own personal management development program at the same time. The rocky transition from sales specialist to corporate generalist was one hurdle. I had a tendency to think in sales terms, and I was tempted to go back and tell my successor how to run marketing. But he was doing a good job. Besides, if I were still preoccupied with my old department, I would be acting as vice president, not as president.

I had to find out what was going on in every area of the company. But the company had grown too big for the office-chat method of fact finding. So I got together with my staff and set up a series of meetings that formed the basis for an internal communications program that we are still following. Every morning from eight-thirty to nine I sit down for a private talk with one of the five vice presidents to learn what's going on in his area and to discuss his problems.

At first, the vice presidents tried putting off on me the final responsibility for making their decisions. My standard reply was, "You've got the facts—you decide." I took the opportunity to make it clear that I expected executives to make their own decisions. They seemed pleased to know that I didn't plan to run their departments.

Once a month, generally before a board meeting, I sit down with the vice presidents for a prod-the-president session. The vice presidents tell me what they want me to pass on to the directors—and what they want me to get from the board in support of their projects. For the record, minutes are typed and filed.

I also get reports on meetings I cannot attend. Public Relations, for example, meets every six weeks and sends its reports to me. Executives from other departments meet weekly and send me summaries. This saves me from having to attend some of these meetings myself.

From the day I became president, there has never been time enough to do all the things I want to do. The standard solution is to work longer hours, but I've been down that dead end before. Besides, time has been a problem throughout the company. It is a problem with two faces. Some people don't have enough time; others waste time. We put a stopwatch on an executive secretary and found she was idle 55 percent of her working day. This excluded time away from her desk for lunch, coffee breaks, and visits to the powder room. She was very busy on personal phone calls.

I turned the time study on myself, hopefully setting the example for the rest of the company. I examined all the things I was doing and realized that I had not yet answered the real question: What *should* I be doing as president?

I should, of course, be doing the eight-to-five, Monday-to-Friday part of the job. That was pretty well under control. But I had just started giving serious attention to (1) developing key people and (2) planning the company's future. This is what I call the big-think part of the job. The question now became: How do I get rid of other things so I will have time to do the big thinking?

The answer began with delegation of some of my routine duties, a streamlining of my personal work schedule, and the appointment of an administrative assistant. I selected a young man in the accounting department who had an excellent background—and who knew the company and the business. He is more than a traditional assistant. Besides screening mail and making appointments, he frequently represents me in the field. On one occasion, for example, he went to Salt Lake City with basic agreements for the purchase of a bottling plant. He set up the contract, hired attorneys, put the finishing touches on negotiations, then brought the contract back for my signature.

I streamlined my daily work schedule by setting up an appointment system. Too often, especially during my first months on the job, people felt free to drop in and say hello. I enjoy talking; so those visits sometimes stretched to 30 or 40 minutes. Meanwhile, outside my office, members of the staff waited, understandably impatient. Now my door is still open, but everyone needs an appointment to get through. Staff members, in particular, like the idea. They get in to see me without wasting so much of their time waiting outside.

The office is a fine place for day-to-day activities, but it's not the best place for big thinking. Even when the door is closed, I always have the feeling that something I should know about is going on outside at the secretary's desk. My favorite thinking spot is a cottage at a nearby lake. When I go to think, I go alone. My wife is beginning to understand. Letting the imagination wander through scraps of ideas can be a stimulating form of recreation. It can also produce useful results.

I often read that being president is the loneliest job in the world. I believed that statement even before I knew why it was true. Now I *know* why. A president can have the best advice and all the facts he needs—but, when it comes to making a decision, he's on his own. The responsibility for the decision, right or wrong, is his.

I saw what this responsibility was like when I was appointed to the board of directors in 1963 and watched my predecessor in action. Serving as a director is indispensable training for the executive who may someday face the board as president.

Most men aren't really surprised when they are appointed president. But few seriously start thinking like presidents until it happens. Only a president thinks like a president.

Toward a New Quality
of Leadership

Clarence Francis

In a few short decades, the art of modern management has virtually attained the status of an established science. Its fast-growing body of knowledge has until now claimed most of our attention, rightfully so. But we must recognize today that the mastery of techniques alone will not sufficiently equip us to meet all the challenges of the future.

The time has come, in fact, to take a new view of our responsibilities. We know, of course, that it is our first duty to conduct our enterprises productively and profitably. We

CLARENCE FRANCIS was, before his retirement, Chairman of the Board, General Foods Corporation. Previously he had been President of the company.

know also that, in apportioning the results of increased productivity, we must maintain balance among the interests of consumers, employees, investors, government, and the community. Our success is measured, indeed, by the extent to which we provide the greatest possible service to the greatest number of people.

Yet we can no longer take for granted the national climate in which we have operated heretofore. I refer not only to the fact that our American system of competitive enterprise faces constant scrutiny, criticism, and pressure for change. This has long been so. But today we find that a new complexity, an atmospheric change, has entered into the relationship of business to the other major elements of the national community: Ours is now a nation perpetually at war. Consequently, national security has become a fixed feature of the economic scene.

One of the goals of our adversary in this war is the depletion of our economic strength. The source of that strength, and indeed the source of our national liberty, is our free, competitive enterprise system. As its custodians, we have a duty to preserve, strengthen, and improve this system in every way we can.

Now, the psychology of a nation at war is made up of many factors, both good and bad. Among these is a continuous air of emergency, which is often desirable, but there is also, all too often, a tendency to expediency. In the presence of these factors, the delicate balance among the several elements of our national life—the economic, the governmental, and the military—may easily be damaged or even destroyed. And this can come about if the leadership of any one element becomes overly dominant while another becomes overly dependent, venal, or weak.

Our new responsibilities, then, in the national atmosphere of today, demand a quality of business leadership much broader than any we have previously envisioned. This leadership must be not only economic but moral, not only practical but spiritual.

Business management, thus viewed, is not just a way of making a living. It is a public trust. Our great economic system will remain strong only as long as we understand its real meaning in the world of today. We must distinguish constantly between apparent success and genuine excellence, between procedure and principle, between mere ambition and a real sense of purpose. Procedures can often be compromised, principles never. To be truly successful every business must operate as a dynamic source of national strength—a productive, profitable, and honorable force—in the world fight for freedom.

In striving toward this goal, business and government must come to a new understanding, for neither can win liberty's war alone. Only the combined best leadership of both, cooperating on the highest plane, can do the job.

Leadership profits from association. We will gain by developing together the qualities so urgently needed in these times—initiative, integrity, decision, judgment, and human understanding. To these I would add the great intangible, faith. For it is fundamentally a faith which we, by uniting, profess—faith in our mission, faith in the future, and faith in our country and the moral and spiritual principles for which our country stands.

Speaking from a faith which the years have fully confirmed, I am confident that we will develop a quality of leadership more than equal to the challenge of today and tomorrow.

Executive Capacity: Leadership? Vision? Judgment?

1. *The Ability to Create a Harmonious Whole*

Crawford H. Greenewalt

IT SEEMS to me that the attributes which make a successful executive are found more than anywhere else in the intangibles. A job analysis, useful enough in other areas, fails

CRAWFORD H. GREENEWALT is at present Chairman, Finance Committee, E. I. duPont de Nemours & Company. Previously he was DuPont's President.

33

completely in appraising executive potential, for the duties defy classification or description.

Most studies agree that an essential quality is leadership, and I have no doubt that it is, in fact, an important executive attribute. But, while leadership is important, I am not at all sure that it is more than a small fraction of the answer.

Judgment is important. Vision is undoubtedly essential. And we could exhaust our list of virtues without reaching the core of the problem. I have known men with leadership, with judgment, with vision. But many of them were not in any sense of the word "good" executives.

The best I can offer is to say that the basic requirement of executive capacity is the ability to create a harmonious whole out of what the academic world calls dissimilar disciplines. This is a fancy way of saying that an executive is good when he can make a smoothly functioning team out of people with the many different skills required in the operation of a modern business. His most important function is to reconcile, to coordinate, to compromise, and to appraise the various viewpoints and talents under his direction so that each individual contributes his full measure to the business at hand in the organization.

During the past century, businesses have grown in size and complexity; research and technical innovation have become essential elements in insuring corporate success; government regulations relating to business conduct have become more numerous and more difficult; and product lines have become bewilderingly diverse.

In short, all the elements of doing business in the twentieth century have increased so much in variety and complexity that their direction is beyond the grasp of a single individual, no matter how gifted he may be. Business has become a team effort, and the task of leadership is no longer simply to possess outstanding competence in one or more areas. The main task of leadership is to deal with many sorts of individuals and to insure high competence in all the new fields. Above all, business leadership must see to it that the many specialized practitioners perform as a harmonious group dedicated to a common objective.

I think the problems encountered by the conductor of a symphony orchestra are analogous to those of a modern business leader. A good conductor need not be able to play the bassoon or the trumpet or the bass viol, but he must recognize the potential of each instrument and the character of each performer. He must deal with them in such a way as to produce a harmonious and effective ensemble.

In the same sense, a business leader need not have expertise in science or in law or in marketing, but he must understand the significance of each. He must know and be able to measure the capacities of the individuals in these various fields. And he must acquire the spiritual qualities that will induce people under his direction to put forth their best efforts in the interests of the enterprise as a whole.

The extent to which an executive succeeds in getting that extra effort is the real measure of his leadership capacity.

2. *And the Greatest of These Is Integrity*

Lyndall F. Urwick

THE modern chief executive in a large corporation is the center of a network of interdependent and interacting social groups. Each and every one of these groups and, as far as possible, the individuals of which they are composed demands his interest and his attention. Neglect of any one of them may do serious hurt to the corporation.

Each one of these groups is in a state of active development, changing and evolving all the time. The whole com-

LYNDALL F. URWICK is now Director (formerly Chairman of the Board), Urwick, Orr & Partners Ltd., London.

plex is in the midst of one of the most profound revolutions in human history—the changeover from a handicraft economy of small units governed by custom to a power-driven economy based on the physical sciences and consisting of almost incomparably larger units. We are still in the middle of the Industrial Revolution. And both the scope and the speed of change are growing and accelerating.

The executive's task is therefore complex and of great social significance. Each of these interacting social groups is composed of individual human beings. Any single one of them who becomes seriously dissatisfied with his group *may* possess personal qualities which will serve to frustrate the common purpose or even to destroy the group altogether.

The great economic enterprises of the present day demand a refinement of social discipline which, in a handicraft age, was unnecessary and unimagined. At the same time, it is a basic tenet of the American dream that no demand for social discipline, whether from the state, the community, or the business corporation, should be allowed to handicap the individual from realizing the full potential of which he is personally capable. In this context, the chief executive is faced with a dilemma.

What help can he expect from science in attempting to solve it? To judge by the analogy from medicine, which has taken many centuries to achieve its present level of sophistication, there seems little prospect that within the lifetime of anyone now living we shall have sufficiently exact knowledge of many aspects of individual human behavior to supersede experienced judgment. The prospect of exact knowledge about human group behavior is much more remote. We have, however, the whole pageant of human experience of administration, much of it as yet little explored from the standpoint of the management issues involved.

Human beings, faced with a complex and significant task about which they lack exact knowledge, are compelled, in the nature of things, to try to simplify the issues involved. One of the most misleading simplifications is the idea that men work for money. But men have all kinds of wants for things that are not material. And, once the basic physical needs are satisfied, these other wants take a leading place in the hierarchy of human motives.

Profit is another misleading simplification. Of course profitability is essential if a business enterprise is to survive. But the idea that it may not survive is usually remote from the minds of the majority of its employees. And to expect them to become enthusiastic about realizing a profit in which they do not participate directly is poor psychology.

An added danger in both these simplifications is that they incline men to be cynical. Everyone knows the phrases —"Money talks," "The almighty dollar," "I am not in business for my health." But few men work well for a cynic. They work wholeheartedly only with a man who himself believes wholeheartedly in them and in what they are trying to do together.

Wholehearted belief by members of a group in what they are trying to do together, combined with reasonable satisfaction as to their treatment as individuals, adds up to what is known as morale. The existence of high morale in any human group is an assurance that individual members will pursue its aims with energy, enthusiasm, and unity and will, to the necessary degree, subordinate personal aims which may conflict with it to the group purpose. The quality in individuals in positions of authority which stimulates morale in their associates is known as leadership.

Many distinctively different personalities have been successful as leaders in different situations. Nevertheless, they have usually been found to possess certain basic qualities in common. Field Marshal Viscount Slim, formerly governor general of Australia, some years ago isolated five qualities almost always found in successful leaders. They were courage, willpower, flexibility of mind, knowledge, and "the fifth quality, on which all the other qualities depend, integrity—the thing that makes people trust you."

Integrity is *the* quality essential in a manager. To convince all the members of all the interlocking groups of which he is the focal point of his integrity and, at the same time, by his foresight and his energy, to protect the corporation and its future when he will have passed on are the cardinal duties which "the law of the situation" imposes on the modern chief executive. If he is to discharge them effectively he needs, above all, two things—faith in what the corporation is trying to do and good faith toward all those associated with him in doing it.

Every President Needs Standards of Performance

Charles E. Spahr

Progress needs planning, but planning—no matter how carefully thought out—does not guarantee progress. It also requires solid policies, sound organization, effective controls based on measurement and inspection, and—particularly important—standards of performance.

Standards are of much greater value if they are applied and used throughout the company. That is why I believe that every executive—including the chief executive—should have standards of performance.

Many presidents feel that to impose standards upon themselves is to limit their flexibility, to expose them to the

Charles E. Spahr is President and Chief Executive Officer of The Standard Oil Company (Ohio).

scrutiny of subordinates, or to demean their position. Presidents, they say, should be above judging. My reaction to such arguments is that these presidents are simply wary of being judged objectively on how well they are performing their job. Presidents *should* be judged. They should, in fact, be judged more critically than any other executives.

Because the chief executive is responsible—through his board of directors—to stockholders, the first and foremost criterion on which his performance should be judged is the company's rate of return. Of the two valid measurements—return on stockholders' investment and return on borrowed and invested capital—I prefer the latter. A president, however, must also be judged on other aspects of performance, including what he does to make sure that his company is growing and preparing for changes in consumer buying habits, technology, and world conditions.

If a president's performance is judged only on the company's rate of return, I can easily imagine a situation in which he succeeds for ten years and then suddenly fails. This may happen, not merely because the rate of return drops, but more important—and often more difficult to detect—because he fails to do all the things that will assure his company's growth through the next ten years and beyond. By then, of course, it is too late, and the company and the stockholders must suffer the consequences.

Effective use of standards of performance for the president is one way to help make sure that such disasters do not occur. By and large, it is the best way. Standards keep the president on his toes. They force him to be both imaginative and sound, daring and prudent.

Standards first filtered into Sohio in the mid-1950's, when our manufacturing department, followed by transportation and purchasing, began to adopt them on an individual, voluntary basis. Although they brought advantages to the functioning of these departments, standards did not become part of company policy until after I became chief executive officer in 1959.

I was not particularly committed to standards at that time, either for myself or for any other executive. I was, however, firmly committed to planning, and my close associates and I began to analyze our corporate position. This critical review convinced me that we needed formalized long-range planning to supplement the 18-month operating plans and 3-year financial plans we had long been preparing.

We also needed better-organized and expanded corporate policy statements. And we needed them in writing so that there would be no misunderstanding about our aims or our methods. We assigned the responsibility for developing a corporate policy manual to my assistant.

At that time, we had job descriptions and salary ranges for all positions, including my own. We decided to supplement these top management job descriptions with guides that would emphasize interdepartmental relationships and spell out delegation of authority. We called them management guides. We now have them for each upper-level executive, including myself, as well as for the board of directors and the executive committee.

The next step was inevitable. We had to establish some

written norms to evaluate the degree to which we were adhering to our plans, policies, and management guides. So, in the spring of 1960, we tackled the problem of standards.

There were three ways to go about instituting standards: from the bottom up; from the top down; or simultaneously, everyone at the same time. Because I was convinced that the president should have them, and because I knew that my example would impress upon all executives and employees the seriousness with which we were going ahead on standards, I decided to begin from the top down. My own standards of performance were worked out first in a series of meetings with all the corporate officers.

As I look back to those meetings, three simple but fundamental rules emerge: (1) Recognize that standards are statements of conditions that will exist when a job is satisfactory. (2) Keep the standards as specific and verifiable as possible, but don't forgo a standard because it isn't readily measurable. And (3) get started right at the beginning on the single most important step in establishing standards for the chief executive or anyone else in the company—getting them down on paper.

By the end of 1960, my standards were more or less polished, and we presented them for approval to the board of directors. I revised my standards in 1962 as conditions changed, and then again in 1964 and 1968. Over all, they represent a continuity, and they were always—as they are now—as verifiable as possible.

They include the statement that satisfactory performance has been attained with respect to return on borrowed and invested capital when the actual rate of return for a year is equal to or exceeds the approved specific objective for that year. Each year the board sets that objective—in writing—as high as possible in the light of anticipated conditions. We have certain criteria below which the objective cannot be set.

Here are other statements from my standards:

- Satisfactory performance has been attained with respect to financial strength when working capital is adequate but not excessive as measured monthly by maintenance of a ratio of current assets to current liability of at least 1.5 to 1 and not more than 2.5 to 1, and when cash and equivalent at the end of each month exceeds 50 percent of the average monthly sales and operating revenue for the preceding 12 months.
- Satisfactory performance has been attained with respect to financial latitude and flexibility so long as the capital structure of the company permits a free choice as to types of new financing. To permit such a choice, the common stock equity of the company should not fall below 70 percent of the total borrowed and invested capital of the company as shown by the statement of financial position.

In general, my standards break down into eight segments: financial results and resources, policy development and administration, planning and investment, organization and management development, corporate security, internal communications, stockholder relations, and public relations. To be sure, not every one of these segments is verifiable. For example, under public relations, the requirement that "key managers take an active role in public affairs" is a rather difficult standard to measure.

One of the statements in my standards requires that each executive who reports to the president shall have standards of performance that have been approved by the president. This means that every vice president has to develop standards. He does so with my help. Furthermore, each vice president is aided by his own subordinates in setting up his standards.

Naturally, in their own standards, the vice presidents also insert a statement requiring standards from their subordinates. Thus standards begin working down through the company ranks. With my approval and firm support, we have had workshop sessions to help all executives develop their own standards—with the cooperation of their superior and subordinates.

A workshop operates like this: Under the guidance of the director of corporate training, an executive whose standards are being developed sits down with his subordinates and, often, his superior. The director begins by explaining what standards are and then has the participants write down every statement applicable to the executive's job that they think is important. Next, they compare statements and work out any discrepancies. At this point, the training director works with the executive to make his standards as specific and verifiable as possible. Finally, the executive's standards of performance are presented to his superior for approval.

As a result of these workshops, we now have standards of performance for executives throughout the organization. With these standards, a man knows what is expected of him and how he will be judged. And he expects to be compensated according to how well he meets his standards.

This is as true for me as it is in anyone else. Each year I submit a detailed report to the board of directors showing how I have reached (or failed to reach) my standards of performance. If I have surpassed my standards, I expect to be rewarded. If, however, I have fallen short and I cannot produce an explanation that satisfies the board, I expect to be censured. That's the way I want it, and I say that's the way all chief executives should want it.

With top-level standards in operation, I am convinced that our management is functioning better than ever. I don't mean to imply that this is true only because we have adopted standards of performance. I am, however, sure that standards of performance are playing an important role in the company's continuing success.

He Said I Should Act like a President

Earl F. Harris

No DOUBT about it. Sales were up, profits were down—'way down. By summer we knew that 1960 was shaping up as the first year since the Depression that the company would lose money.

As president, I was shocked. What was wrong? We had grown steadily through the postwar years. From 1946 to 1960, sales increased 450 percent, employees 350 percent. But why were we going in the red this year, 1960, with sales at an all-time high?

Determined to find out what was wrong, I gathered our

EARL F. HARRIS is President, Rodney Hunt Co., Orange, Massachusetts.

18-man management group for a series of meetings in a nearby motel. We had some basic problems, all right, but we didn't know exactly what they were or where or how to go about looking for them. In our own crude way we managed to agree that our principal troubles at the moment centered on budgets, indirect costs, and our company pricing policies. It was a start.

I recall looking at the faces around the table and feeling the growing temptation within me to throw in the towel and call in a management consultant. Then I remembered the casual comment of a visitor in my office earlier in the year. "You've got as many top men in a company of this size as I've ever seen," he said. Perhaps, I told myself, we could straighten this out ourselves. This was an opportunity to practice what I had heard others call consultative management. Draw on the strengths and skills of your management team, they had said. It was worth a try to test the basic philosophy.

So each man in charge of a cost center picked three other managers to help him explore the problems of his center and to come up with possible solutions. These managers were to advise and consult only. All decisions were to be made exclusively by the cost-center manager responsible. I had no intention of sponsoring committee-style decision making.

As manager in charge of the administrative cost center, I selected three managers for my consulting team and got down to business. What happened next came at one of our meetings. I don't recall who made the remark, but someone looked straight at me and said: "Things would be better if the president acted more like a president."

I honestly don't remember my reaction at that moment. I probably went on with the meeting, telling myself that in a weak moment I had let a subconscious thought sneak by. But someone had made the remark, and I had heard it. What did it mean? I didn't know exactly, but I had a suspicion. A few days later I packed a suitcase and drove to a motel where I could take a long, close look at myself—both as a man and as president of Rodney Hunt.

The present was clear and cruel enough. The company was in the red, and an executive staff member had seriously questioned my competence. What about people outside the company? What did they think? I asked friends and bankers who knew me and the company. There were no bouquets for either of us.

The short-term future promised its share of problems, too. Employees were voting in November on whether or not to join a union. The Christmas bonus was definitely out. And neither employees nor family stockholders were very happy about the new equipment expenditures or the new company plane soon to be delivered.

I looked to the past for some encouraging signs. My education included Dartmouth College, Worcester Polytech, and Babson Institute of Business Administration before the war and engineering studies at the University of Virginia during my Army service. I came back to the family business in Orange, Massachusetts, in 1946, the silver-spoon son of the president and major stockholder, a dynamic man with 99 patents to his name who had seen Rodney Hunt through a depression and two major floods. The following year I became vice president and a director.

In those days we had a 22-month backlog on orders for textile machinery, our main product line. Prices were subject to "price at delivery time." It was difficult to make enough mistakes to wipe out profits.

My father wanted me to learn his job as fast as possible. I had a lot to learn. In many ways, he was ahead of his time in the world of New England textiles. He had foreseen the decline of natural fibers and the rise of synthetics during the 1930's, and he had put the company in the good technical hands of textile-school graduates. He welcomed new products and new markets, and he delegated more authority than you might expect from a typical New England businessman. He had no sympathy with finance, though. When I negotiated a bank loan, he warned me: "Careful, Earl, or the bankers will be running the business."

My early career had its bright spots and its blunders, with my father backing me up—right or wrong. I jangled the nerves of top management by some unwise juggling of boxes on the organization chart, but I straightened that mess out. On the credit side, I strengthened the sales function and took steps to broaden the product line to correct our unhealthy dependence on the textile industry—our principal customer.

Although my father was still president in title, I was, in fact, running the company as a one-man show and doing a reasonably good job. The company doubled in size from

1946 to 1951, and so did the base of our future troubles. Through the 1950's I sat through just about every management course and seminar in the catalog. I began to really learn something about the difficult art of management and to do some experimenting, too.

In 1955, I formed a 12-man management team to help pinpoint company problems and to suggest solutions. I looked rather proudly upon this use of group dynamics as a step toward professional management—as I understood it then. What we really had was simply an information meeting. I told people what I had decided; then I asked for their comments. Most sessions ended with my critics bowed and silenced and my hand somewhat sore from pounding the table.

By that time, many of our top managers—men who had 30 and 40 years with the company—had retired. Without a reserve of up-and-coming young executives to fall back on, we tried to fill the gaps. We hired new people with enthusiasm, quickly became disenchanted with them and fired them. It was mainly my fault. I had hired the wrong men. I didn't really know what I expected from them, and I guess they didn't either.

But there were bright spots, too. Between 1951 and 1956, the company grew 50 percent. Back in 1948, our markets were within 300 miles of the plant. We were now selling worldwide, with exports accounting for 20 percent of sales. We had new products to sell, and they were being turned out on modern equipment. Those few remaining old machines—still belt-driven from the ceiling—were now subjects for nostalgia and a reminder to older employees of the company that was. And, despite our internal troubles—or perhaps because of them—we gradually became organization-minded, taking our first steps toward management development based on a program of selection and training.

In 1956, I became president in title as well as deed. In 1957, our year of peak volume and employment, we began holding quarterly information meetings for plant employees. We thought they would be glad to know they were working for a profitable company. But the uneasy shuffle of feet and the undisguised yawns at plant meetings soon taught us to be brief and to the point. No details, please, just the bare facts.

In 1958, we discovered the cost-center concept. Each manager was made responsible for his center. At the same time, I began to hold monthly review meetings with our vice president–treasurer (my brother Ed), our vice president–marketing, and the manager whose function we happened to be discussing. These men later became the core of our consultative management team. We even talked casually about long-range five-year plans, but they remained blue-sky blueprints for another four years.

So there I stood on the eve of 1960. Thus far, I had successfully taken a small family company through a period of hectic but profitable growth. The company had many strong points and some weak ones, too. I was one of the weak points.

In the spring of 1960, my father died. By early summer, I knew we were going into the red. The combination of events shocked me—first into thought, then into action. My father's death had removed my personal bench mark. While he was alive, I had tried to please him, to deserve his respect. Now he was gone, and I asked myself: "For *whom* am I trying to do my job?" That's when I drove off to that motel for a long talk with myself.

I realized that while my father was alive I had not really been the chief executive—either in mind or in manner. I never really felt the full responsibility of the position. I was abdicating rather than delegating authority by assigning responsibility without inspecting the results. And I was spending more time and energy in operating details than in management processes.

I heard and saw nothing except what I wanted to see and hear, and I did everything I could myself. I was really the product manager most of the time, running all over the world, taking people with me, looking at new products, negotiating, hiring salesmen.

I began to understand why our 12-man management group had never really worked out. I had sincerely wanted to build a management team in which people at all levels of the company would do their own problem solving. This meant encouraging and drawing on the talents and skills of others. I had actually been building an authority-obedience system in which these very qualities were being stilled—if not killed off outright.

I had been fascinated by the small but deadly traps in management. I had wasted time second-guessing my executives in their own areas, questioning their decisions, or telling them in detail how to carry out their projects. I had tolerated mistakes and accepted excuses for failure, frequently even making excuses for them. And I constantly got sucked into the morass of operating details.

With regret, I recall getting clobbered several times on decisions that rightfully belonged to others. It was difficult for me to say, "Go ahead. That's your job and your decision." I was tending shop instead of running it.

There were times when I sat around the table with other company executives at management seminars and read all kinds of things into their simple questions. "Is it a family business?" or, "Are you the son of the owner?" Then I would start apologizing—to myself, at least—for being the kid with the silver spoon in his mouth.

At the same time, I was telling myself that if I did my job well I had as much right to be president as the fellow who started his own business or who worked his way up without the breaks. Besides, there were a lot of good family businesses being run professionally. I decided that I wanted the challenge and responsibility of being president.

But, I asked myself, "What is my responsibility as president?" "How does a man act like a president?" I simply had not faced the question squarely. My responsibility as president was to run my company professionally—for a profit. (Easier said than done.) It was my responsibility to get all areas of company management to work together to reach this goal. (That's why I turned to consultative management.)

As I worked to improve the performance of the company and its executives, I turned to the task of improving my own performance as president. What should I be doing as president? To find out, I looked at the position descriptions of other presidents. Using them as guides, I went on to write my own workable but nonremarkable six-point description. My basic responsibilities became to (1) establish company objectives, (2) develop policies, (3) build and maintain an efficient organization, (4) install controls, (5) prepare short- and long-range programs of action, and (6) represent the company before the public, industry, and government. To advise and consult with me in carrying out my responsibilities, I set up a permanent five-man top management group consisting of myself and the managers of our four basic functions—finance, marketing, engineering and controls, and manufacturing.

The first year under the reign of consultative management was devoted to putting out brush fires that were eating up our profits. Job descriptions helped us discover that we had surplus people and that we were harboring many cases of job duplication. (Each department head said the other departments had the surplus people.) Example: We were keeping two inventories, each under a different foreman. Solution: Combine them into a single inventory under the foreman for production scheduling.

We also found serious looseness in our estimating, purchasing, and pricing policies. Example: We had sold and shipped a $1,600 replacement part for $1,000. Solution: Pinpoint responsibility and authority in the organization for estimating and pricing.

An inflexible price policy imposed on our field salesmen had been cutting into sales. From this discovery came our "best price" policy to help salesmen meet competition. A revamp of the purchasing setup saved us 10 percent on certain materials during the first year alone. We even discovered—much to our surprise—that we could save money by discontinuing some so-called essential service products without a whimper from customers.

Cutting surplus employees was another story. It was difficult to ask a supervisor to lay off a neighbor, his bowling mate, or the father of his son's best friend. That's what often happened. It was bound to in a town of 6,500 people. But it had to be done.

Proof that we were on the right path showed up in 1961. Business was down slightly; profits were up. Why? There was no boom market, we offered no new products, and there were no management heroes or new men in key jobs. Very simply, the performance of people had improved; specifically, management people—myself included.

Our strategy of tackling cost-reduction problems through closely knit four-man cost-center teams was paying off. As we shifted our attention to longer-range problems, the five-man top management group began laying the groundwork for our first five-year objectives. After three months of study, we came up with corporate financial objectives for 1962–1966 that backed our decision to become a growth company. Our yardstick became a growth of net worth, replacing percentage of profit on sales as the measure of how well we are doing.

Our objectives stated that Rodney Hunt would retain profits after taxes to afford an annual growth of net worth of 7.5 percent per year (better than industry average). Corporate objectives were backed with targets for contribution to profit for each of the four product divisions. (You should have heard the beefs, at first.) Each division head, in turn, submitted a detailed one-year plan for reaching his target. Our criteria for these targets spelled out that they should be attainable and challenging. (More beefs.) Like a chain reaction, targets emerged right down the line for orders, new business, shipments. Each area knew what it was expected to contribute as its share of profits to the overall corporate goal.

Our first attempt at planning was a good start, but it was too short-term. We missed our shipments in 1963 simply because we hadn't put enough details into the second year of the plan. We remedied this defect in our second five-year corporate plan, which is taking us through 1969.

Discovering the importance of planning and practicing the textbook techniques of group participation didn't come easy. At first, division heads resisted our efforts to sit down for three or four days to talk about division plans for three years ahead. If their bodies were with us at the table, their minds too often were back in the shop figuring ways to meet this month's orders. We had a lot to learn.

I used to come back from management seminars in New York full of enthusiasm only to face a stone wall when I told people about the management ideas I had picked up. They simply didn't know what I was talking about. They didn't know the language of professional management—the language I was just beginning to understand.

I told myself that if we wanted to create a company atmosphere in which consultative management would work, then we would have to expose managers to the same ideas. So we started sending our people—right down to the supervisor's level—to management sessions in New York. And we still do today. Results have been encouraging. Learning the importance of planning, for example, has helped us develop an immunity to that dread disease—management by crisis. Our meetings are improving, and so is the quality of our decisions. All this didn't happen overnight. We went through two tough years before we really learned how to run meetings—the heart of consultative management.

Four principles stand out in running meetings. The president must (1) believe in people, (2) learn to listen, (3) develop personal skills in conference leadership, (4) make the decisions. I discovered the hard way that consultative management doesn't relieve you of your decision-making responsibility.

To improve our meetings, we even held meetings about our meetings. As standard procedure, we closed each session of the five-man management group with a ten-minute appraisal period. Did we achieve the purpose of the meeting? Did everyone contribute? If not, why not? This face-to-face feedback really works.

There are signs that consultative management is beginning to take a foothold at lower management levels of the company. Several years ago we built a half-million-dollar plant with the help of foreman-level teams. After one meeting, a machine-shop foreman even called in his subforeman and chewed him out for "not contributing" during the session. The plant cost less than budgeted, and it was completed far ahead of schedule. And we later had the same gratifying experience with our new foundry.

Some significant changes have taken place in the company. Our five-man inside board of directors that met once a year for routine approvals has been replaced by a six-man mixed board. Insiders include myself, the vice president–treasurer, and the vice president–marketing. Outsiders include the long-range planner for a major corporation, an attorney, and the president of a company that has been through problems similar to ours.

In addition, an information center built around a computer is now in operation, providing sales, marketing, and other data to back up our planning.

The most important development, however, goes back to our management briefing in December 1963. It ended with a strong feeling that one of our prime problems was communication. To many of the 29 managers at the briefing, communication meant policy statements, reports, and memos. To me, communication is essentially attitudes, not contents or mechanics.

To improve our company communication we asked a consultant to set up and run a companywide sensitivity training program. The positive results have astounded us all. From vice presidents down to foremen, there is a new atmosphere in the company. Managers who too often worked together in a state of hostility are putting their conflicts on the table. Instead of suppressing their interpersonal problems, managers are confronting them squarely and resolving them—to their own personal benefit and the company's too.

There has been, for example, a marked improvement in the working relationships between engineering and sales people—those traditional intracompany rivals. Each side appreciates the contribution of the other. There are fewer villains in the company and more managers with similar problems.

That attitudes are changing for the better is also proved by the growing effectiveness of our consulting team at all levels. It is encouraging to see new strength developing in people. And that, of course, is one of the primary responsibilities of management.

The record speaks for itself. Rodney Hunt is a far better, more profitable company today than in 1960. As for myself, am I a better president?

I often think back to that meeting in 1960 when, in response to my associate's quip, I began asking myself, "How do you act like a president?" I am still trying to find the answer, but I know that it has to do with a management philosophy of providing direction and developing people. Progress at Rodney Hunt verifies this.

The Company That Runs in Circles: An Experiment in Participative Management

John W. Joanis

I STARTED thinking in circles in 1964, the year I became executive vice president of Sentry and made a systematic tour of our 40 branch offices. Some veteran field executives were startled because my visits hadn't been cleared through the procedural labyrinth. The standard communication pattern was to talk up to a superior or down to subordinates. I was communicating diagonally across the company without going through the corporate chain of command.

JOHN W. JOANIS is President, Sentry Insurance, Stevens Point, Wisconsin.

At the time, Sentry Insurance was growing at a sluggish 3 percent a year. In many ways, the company was a sleeping giant dreaming about better, bygone days. My mandate from the board of directors: Make Sentry an industry leader once again.

Sentry had become a rigid, authoritarian company ruled by manuals that ground out the details of every job, even down to what to do if you'd lost your company-issue pencil. Everyone punched a time clock: clerks, the controller, even the president. Bells rang out the start and finish of the working day, lunch hours, even coffee breaks. People and their responsibilities were fitted into precise little boxes, neatly stacked into that pyramid called the Sentry organization chart.

Hundreds of capable, well-trained employees were numbed by the system. It kept them from stretching their skills and working at their full potential. I soon discovered, however, that it hurts when blood begins to flow back into a numbed limb.

We wanted our people to think in terms of working with others on mutually agreed-on tasks. Involving them in setting objectives and planning the company's future, we hoped, would get them to raise their personal sights and become truly excited about Sentry once again. We were really introducing participative management. But we didn't know the concept by that name at the time.

To get people out of the boxes, we began to talk about circles of overlapping responsibility. The circle concept was admittedly a device at this stage—and a rather crude one at that. It was used to demonstrate how each manager's functions intertwine and overlap en route to common corporate goals. It seemed to defy the management tradition that "a man must have only one boss" or "everybody must have a precise, well-defined assignment."

Three concentric circles illustrate our basic idea of each employee's triple responsibility. First, he is responsible for his own function. That's the inner circle. Second, he is responsible for working with functions related to his own. That's the second circle. Third, he is responsible to the total company, Sentry Insurance. That's the big circle.

Our plans for Sentry's future growth were presented at each stop on the 40-office tour, which came to be known as Operation Aircade. Sentry is on the move, I told our people. We need your enthusiasm and support, your ideas and reactions.

At the same time, I announced that Sentry would be doing $1 billion a year in premium sales by the time I retired—1983. This was a reversion to the old technique of setting objectives from the top without involving others. But that wasn't the reason the announcement created a mild sensation. Our premium sales were headed for $133 million that year, and $1 billion looked like the moon or beyond. There was a general state of shock when I told people we were going to reach that goal by encouraging people with more talent than they were using—and with more ambition than management recognized—to outgrow their jobs. We wanted them to take a more active role in setting objectives. This, we hoped, would develop in them a sense of personal commitment to Sentry's long-term growth objectives.

The old chain-of-command system had to go. Communication was the key. We would have to communicate not only up and down but across and diagonally—as I had done on my branch-office tour. We needed new ideas and criticism.

There was, at first, the inevitable employee resistance. "Write it down so we can see it," they pleaded at employee meetings called to outline our new approach. But how can you set down commandments for a concept that is constantly in motion?

You can't expect people to come out of their boxes if they're boxed into a nine-to-five operation; so we threw out the time clocks. (That was a popular move.) But we reverted to the old management techniques again when I personally set down the targets for the first year, then sat back and awaited the results of Project '64. I counted on the energy and enthusiasm created by Operation Aircade to make it all come true. It didn't.

Project '64 surpassed its goal of $133 million in premiums by $3 million but fell woefully short of the $5 million surplus (profit) goal. We cleared only $633,000.

Project '65 showed considerable improvement. We targeted $142 million in premiums and brought in $145 million. The surplus target was $5 million; we made $2.3 million.

For the first time we had set up timetables and brought

in regional office managers to help establish objectives they would have to live with. The objectives called for an annual growth rate of 11.4 percent and an eventual 10 percent after-tax return. Actually, we were looking for a slow, steady improvement in profits. The 10-percent return was targeted for 1983.

In November 1965, the then chairman of the board announced that the president would become chairman in six months and I would take over as president and chief executive officer. In February 1966, the board asked me to spell out my plan of operation for Sentry. In May, I presented the corporation manifesto for the dynamic changes we planned to make.

We set out to make every objective specific, understandable, quantifiable, and motivational. The long-range 10-percent after-tax objective, for example, would be reached this way: 4 percent from policy underwriting, 6 percent from corporate investments. This meant a new, aggressive investment philosophy for our companies.

Responsibility of the sales force was limited to (1) bringing in new business and reaching premium objectives and (2) improving our retention ratio—keeping a higher proportion of the profitable business we already have. The primary responsibility of marketing was to design our policies, price them, and develop marketing programs—all to assure Sentry a profit on every policy.

A dictum in the old company manual cautioned employees not to use the word "profit" because we are a mutual company. The previous management had dealt almost exclusively in dollar goals, too. The new guidelines we adopted measured growth in percentages, a small but significant change. Even more significant, perhaps, was the push to exceed goals rather than merely reach them on schedule.

Personnel plans called for stepped-up internal training and retraining programs to fulfill our anticipated management needs. The stress was on individual development of many talented people. "Stretch" became the byword. Regional offices became profit centers, and new business opportunities opened up, as we went into new markets and increased our efforts to get larger shares of traditional markets.

The plan also detailed our new organizational structure made up of circles. I am at the center of a large top management circle ringed by 15 vice presidents who head up corporate functions. Surrounding the corporate circle is a ring of circles, one for each of the eight regional vice presidents. Each of these circles, in turn, is orbited by branch office satellites. (See opposite page.)

A circle is essentially a work group composed of managers committed to mutually agreed-on objectives. It operates on the synergistic principle: You can get better results from two people working together on a problem than from two people working separately on the same problem.

When a problem requires the expertise of a man normally outside the group, the circle expands to take in the specialist or any combination of experts. Better decisions result. At the same time, each manager is exposed to other

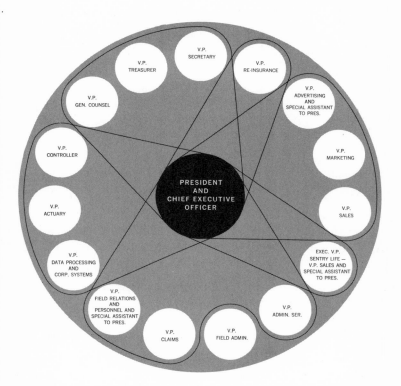

functions which help him develop a total-company, rather than a strictly functional, point of view.

Not every manager can operate effectively in the circular system. Participants must have confidence in themselves and trust in others to direct their energies toward solving problems instead of defending their special interests. Some managers are not yet ready to operate within the circle; some never will be.

The circular concept doesn't mean wishy-washy committee-type management. We share authority, but we don't abdicate responsibility. Each manager is responsible for decisions in his circle. We measure results, mine included.

Most companies proclaim the importance of communication. We stress total communication—free flow in all directions. The personnel vice president spends a major part of his time directing ideas, instructions, information, and reactions from the field to the top management circle and back again.

We hold weekly telephone conferences between headquarters in Stevens Point, Wisconsin, and our regional offices. And we have the usual array of company magazines, posters, and bulletins. But the most effective form of communication is still the face-to-face, person-to-person exchange between supervisor and supervised. Our company jet is a major move toward stepping up face-to-face encounters with field managers and their people—and with less wear and tear on me and members of my staff.

The most significant programs to move Sentry toward genuine participative management were begun in 1966. In August of that year we introduced Operation Mirror—a two-part organizationwide survey in which employees rated their supervisors as managers and Sentry as a company. We tried to learn how Sentry people work together so we could make work situations within the company more satisfying and productive. We also hoped the survey would (1) show the supervisor where his performance could be improved and (2) give him the opportunity to take the necessary steps to improve his managerial skills.

Outside consultants tabulated the findings. Top management got the results of the company part of the survey. Each supervisor received his own rating sheet along with an all-supervisor tally so he could match his score against the corporate composite. Then he was on his own. Most of the supervisors took our suggestion and invited subordinates to sit down in group meetings to discuss their scoring.

Some supervisors asked for further analysis of their ratings to help pinpoint their problem areas. Others wanted additional supervisory and, in some cases, sensitivity training. But, in every case, requests for help were strictly voluntary. Over all, there was little resistance to the program, and there are signs of a marked improvement in supervisory performance at many levels.

Taking the same approach to improve top management performance, I asked our 30 corporate officers to rate each other, using their own categories. Some set up simple number scales, an X marking the score in each category. Others wrote paragraphs.

In private sessions, I asked each officer to explain his evaluations of his fellow officers. Why, for example, did he rate Joe and Harry at the low end of the scale in cooperation? Some backed up their ratings with specific incidents. Others admitted they might not have been objective in their ratings because of difficulties in working with certain officers.

I then showed each officer how his fellow officers had rated him. This disclosure I followed with my personal evaluation of his role on the corporate team. We talked about our working relationships, and I stressed what we could do together to improve his effectiveness as a manager.

Some officers were really worried when they went into the evaluation sessions. Most of them came out better managers and wiser men. They realized that their weaknesses were no secret to others. In most cases, they welcomed the exchange. Just a few years ago we wouldn't have dared to ask for this degree of frankness.

Not everyone took the criticism gracefully. One officer complained that his associates didn't appreciate his difficulty in making a recent shift in assignment. He didn't deny he had problems; he just felt that his peers had been too harsh in evaluating him. The feedback, however, helped this officer spot his main problem areas and prompted him to ask for help.

There were cases where officers were not doing a particularly good job in some areas of their assignments. They didn't know it, but their fellow officers did. The revelations usually led to the realization that they needed training in these areas. Such training was swiftly arranged.

It may be that we occasionally have people in jobs that play up their weaknesses rather than their strengths. Where this is the case, we attempt to find openings in the company that will use rather than frustrate their main talents.

The officer evaluation program is now an annual affair. One year I put the officers in my circle through a what-would-you-do-in-my-chair exercise. What kind of men would you recruit for the board of directors? What kind of company would you run? Are there industry problems that I've missed? What changes would you make?

Some frankly said they didn't want to play the game. They thought I was testing them. But now it's clear to them that I really need their assistance. And they like pointing out problems I may have missed and giving me advice.

Such discussions—as frank and honest as I've been able to make them—help me identify a manager's talents and areas of personal satisfaction. These are important clues in determining how best to use each man in the organization —for both the company's and his own personal benefit.

Recently, for example, the head of a team set up to develop new markets agreed to concentrate on evaluating markets rather than on seeking them out. He has a probing, analytical mind better suited to looking behind and through statistics and other data than to uncovering likely new markets in unlikely places. I'm sure he'll be happier in the new role, and so will we.

Every officer knows whether he is being considered as a possible successor to me. And I tell him why he is or isn't. The circle concept of organization, in this case, is a perfect device for showing a man what skills are required in other positions and functions. It doesn't take long for him to find out whether he has the skills—and the temperament—to be president.

All these programs still haven't completely transformed

Sentry from a rigidly authoritarian company into a model of participative management. I expect it will take a few more years for our new management philosophy to reach into every corner of the organization. But I'm delighted with our progress so far. Results are quietly beginning to show up in the places that count. Running the company in circles obviously pays off.

The Man in Charge of Questions: The President in the Market-Oriented Company

Fortune Peter Ryan

Bᴀᴄᴋ in the old days before modern marketing, companies turned out products that they thought the customers should want. Today's market-oriented company rejects this philosophy in favor of producing and selling products that it *knows* the customers want. This is as it should be, for the first objective of any business is to please its customers and thereby show a profit.

This objective must be kept clearly in view. "Give them

Fᴏʀᴛᴜɴᴇ Pᴇᴛᴇʀ Rʏᴀɴ, at the time he wrote this article, was President, Royal McBee Corporation.

73

what they want" must become the daily guide of every executive in the company. This may seem a trite, even glib, approach, but it overcomes formidable psychological blocks. In finance and accounting, set procedures or traditional approaches may come to be regarded as ends in themselves. Thus they tend to obscure the real aim: to market products that customers want at a realistic and fair price.

Of course, we must not confuse the slogan with the doing. It is up to the chief executive to make sure that every department in the company is geared—individually and collectively—to give the customer what he wants. This, in essence, is integrated marketing—the single most important development in marketing today. And it's up to the chief executive to make sure his company's marketing is built around this concept.

Integration must begin at the operating level, and it must include field selling, advertising, sales promotion and merchandising, and public relations and publicity, as well as finance, engineering, manufacturing, and distribution. There is no hard and fast technique to accomplish this. Some chief executives choose to place the working responsibility with a senior executive such as the marketing vice president; others prefer formal coordinating committees. Still others are fortunate in being able to rely on operating staff heads who have the personality and inclination to work closely together without the aid of any formal organization.

Obviously, the same system will not work for every company. The mechanical means for creating an integrated marketing program, after all, are subordinate to the objective itself, and the chief executive must choose the machinery which best fits his company. Since emotions and other personal factors are involved, he must keep an open mind when working out plans for integrating the marketing effort.

To make this concept work in his company, the president must keep in mind that he has the ultimate responsibility for marketing. He must establish the procedures and the organization, and he must ask the questions that keep his executives on the right track. In short, he is the marketing leader of his company. But note the word "leader." He must not fall into the trap of becoming his own director of marketing, any more than he should assume the daily responsibilities of other functions.

With his overall knowledge of the company and his insight into his industry, the job of coordinating and directing every phase of the marketing effort falls on the president. He is the best judge of whether marketing is on the right track. And, because he's the dominant figure in long-range planning, he's the right man to make sure that marketing is the basis for all planning being done in other corporate areas. This means he must review all of the company activities that have a bearing on marketing.

With these broad responsibilities spelled out, what, then, is the chief executive's precise role in the marketing effort—and what means can he use to carry it out? The Greek philosophers of more than 2,000 years ago defined the problem: Finding the right answer, they pointed out, is not too difficult if someone will shoulder the far more difficult task of asking the right question.

Thus one of the most important roles in marketing for the chief executive is that of chief question asker. This is because he is best equipped to ask the right questions and to sense whether he is getting the right answers. He must look at his company and ask:

- Is research and development producing ideas that lead to products the customer wants, or is the real objective losing out to some fascinating scientific problem?
- Is quality control in engineering, manufacturing, and servicing adhering to the exacting standards that are required to fully satisfy the customer? (The director of quality for both products and services may well report directly to the president. His responsibilities may then run the gamut from the problems of mishandled collection letters to the establishment of standards for the most complicated products.)
- Is pricing determined realistically on the basis of all competitive and cost factors?
- Are distribution and inventory practices geared to marketing requirements and the customer's needs, rather than to the company's convenience?
- Is management manpower being developed so that a vibrant, imaginative marketing program will be assured five or ten years from now?

Some questions the president must ask himself: Am I overawed by a mere mass of factual data in a market research report? Can I sense when some essential facts are missing? Am I correctly interpreting this information in my decision making? And, finally, there is this persistent question: Are our marketing methods and techniques the least costly and the most efficient means of getting our products to the consumer?

Questioning has proved its value as a two-way street, particularly on the marketing firing line. I don't believe a chief executive can escape or delegate the obligation to meet personally with the field sales force and with customers. There is no better way to assess the value of the marketing program than by observing and asking questions at the point where the actual sale is made.

This is no easy task. Yet it is essential, whether the chief executive has come up through the sales ranks or through some other specialty. In fact, it may be even more important when he has come up through marketing and may, therefore, be inclined to believe that he is well up on the field salesman's job. For sales patterns and customer reactions do change. Selling techniques and problems today differ from what they were a year ago or five years ago.

Such personal contacts take time. It is a simple matter to walk down the corridor to talk to your vice president of finance, and it is easy enough to visit a manufacturing plant or a research and development center. A trip into the field for an informal talk with a salesman is much more difficult to arrange—yet the results are well worth the time and trouble.

Visits to the field provide opportunities, as the situation warrants, to offer a man a sincere word of congratulations for a job well done. They enable the chief executive to sense problems that may exist but never show up on a formal sales report. And they also permit him to determine what steps he should take to assure customer satisfaction and, with it, repeat business.

The president should try to find the time to talk to major customers about his company's products and services whenever he has the chance. And, on occasion, he can well take the first step toward meeting the customer with the frank acknowledgment that he would like to help his sales people tell their story. If a closer, more responsive supplier-customer relationship is thereby established, it certainly can be only good for both parties.

All through these contacts, the chief executive must be reflecting back on his company and asking this question: Are we doing everything we can to make our marketing program efficient and profitable? This implies a built-in willingness to change and accept new marketing patterns if better ones come along. And, in turn, this willingness to change means that the president must accept risk as part of the price he pays for encouraging creativity in the company's marketing effort.

The chief executive can, in fact, accomplish a great deal when he is willing to take reasonable, calculated risks and try out new marketing ideas aimed at giving the customer what he wants.

The President's Turn to Listen

W. E. Danner

Sᴏᴍᴇᴛʜɪɴɢ was wrong with our monthly management meetings.

The agenda for each three-day session was always drawn up and distributed in advance. As chairman, I carefully prepared my material; so did the attending members of my management team—all of them competent men.

But the meetings were not producing results. We were wasting time, and members seemed to let their attention wander from the subjects under consideration. Time and time again, at critical moments, someone would throw in a completely new subject. The interruption would generally be introduced with: "I know this isn't the time, but. . . ." These interruptions were ruining our meetings.

W. E. Dᴀɴɴᴇʀ is President, Henry K. Wampole & Company, Limited, Perth, Ontario.

The same thing often happened at the end of a meeting. Just as I would be happily counting our accomplishments, someone would bring up another new subject. Discussion would begin all over again, and our hard-won results would be lost in confusion. Curiously enough, the new subjects would generally be good ones.

What was the problem? It occurred to me that in addition to *my* agenda for the meeting there was another unwritten agenda that I did not know about. My agenda consisted of subjects that *I* wanted to discuss. That unwritten agenda consisted of subjects that *they* wanted to talk about. These concerned the problems that were bothering them. They were bringing them up during the meeting simply to bring them to my attention.

It was these problems—real or imaginary—which were preventing us from having successful meetings. As long as the members felt that their problems would not be given a hearing, that I was not listening, then I was not going to have their complete attention and participation at the meetings.

I tried out an idea. I prepared my agenda as usual. But, instead of distributing it, I listed the subjects to be discussed on the blackboard at the beginning of the meeting —without comment. Then I said, "These are the subjects that I want to talk about. Now I'm going around the table so you can tell me what *you* want to talk about."

I wrote down the subjects as people called them off. I answered some questions on the spot and postponed others for a later meeting. Still others were already on the agenda.

To my surprise, some that were not were more important than some that were. So I added them to the agenda for the meeting that day.

What has happened since? First, and most important, our meetings are better. The members now know that I am aware of their problems, and they also know that their problems are going to be discussed. This has removed the block that was preventing them from fully participating in the meetings. At the same time, the new subjects round out the agenda. And, of course, my role as chairman of the monthly management meeting is now much easier.

The solution was so simple that I wondered why I had not thought of it before. But that was part of the problem. I had not been *listening* to what people were trying to tell me. I discovered that unless a president learns to listen— and listen hard—people won't come up with the good ideas they are capable of. And they won't speak out with the frankness the president needs if he is to know what they really think and what their problems really are.

For example, is a manager's request for a larger staff justified? Does he really need new people, or is he merely trying to build an empire? Or does the request indicate that he has problems in his department and that changes in the way he is running it are in order?

I took my new-found listening skill outside the meeting room and applied it in contacts with all my company people. I soon found myself thinking of them in terms of needs, ambitions, strengths, and weaknesses—not merely as subordinates and employees. By giving them a chance to talk and by listening carefully to their questions and comments, I began to develop an insight into their problems. For the first time, I really began to understand the basis for their objections to some of my proposals and projects. Once I discovered what their real objections were, I was well on my way to winning their full support for my decisions and programs.

As I look back, I see now that all this began to happen the day I discovered the importance of listening.

People—Every Boss's Job

Frederick R. Kappel

Each of us has his own ideas about effective business leadership. For myself, I want to do what I can to create and maintain an atmosphere where useful things get done and people get satisfaction from doing them well. I want the things that are done, and the way they are done, to strengthen the future of the business as well as the present.

All of this goes back to the people in our organizations and how they are handled. This is every boss's job, and certain needs are everywhere fundamental. For instance, bosses must look at people and their work together, not separately. Work must be done well, and the people who

Frederick R. Kappel is a Director and retired Chairman of the Board of American Telephone and Telegraph Company. He also served AT&T as President. Still earlier, he was President of Western Electric Company.

do it must fare well—the two must be in balance. Standards of performance must be clear, not fuzzy; a man needs to know just what he is supposed to do and, later, how well he is judged to have done it.

But, along with these fundamentals, there has to be leadership that will stir people to work to make the business successful, not because they are being pushed, but because they *want* to.

This kind of leadership is many things. It is stating goals that excite people. It is demonstrating personal integrity and setting the personal example. It is putting enthusiasm into the operation. It is communicating both ways—listening as well as talking. It is rewarding merit and penalizing failure or shortcomings, honestly and fairly. It is the right combination of these for any situation—and the situation is always changing.

I think managements need to work constantly to develop these leadership attributes at all levels. I also think that line organizations in big companies need personnel-staff help of particularly high caliber, for it is harder to really know about people and how to lead them than about any other aspect of a business.

The personnel staff have important responsibilities in administering wage practices, pensions, health, and other programs. But this is only part of their job. I think they have another key role, and I want to see them make it increasingly influential.

It seems to me it should be their job to keep looking at all aspects of how we handle people and to come up with sound, thoughtful ideas for doing better. They should be researchers and educators. They should be scanning the horizon and doing the kind of thinking that a busy operating man does not have time for. The operating manager shouldn't have to keep needling them to look at problems and develop solutions. They should be doing them so competently that they will never have trouble commanding respect for their recommendations. In short, their counsel on matters affecting people ought to be the wisest and most sought-after in the company.

The first need, clearly, is for the chief executive and his top management group to *want* a good job and set the example. But—I emphasize again—the second need is for strong, imaginative, practical staff help provided by people who know how to get the necessary knowledge and how to put their recommendations across. Like all staff work, theirs should be a continuous effort to revise and renew tradition, to keep pumping new life into it. In fact, this concept applies particularly to the handling of people, for here we are dealing with the human factors that create the tradition.

Be an Amateur Psychologist—
But Be a Good One

Alfred J. Marrow

I want to take issue with the popular phrase "Don't be an amateur psychologist." I suggest that as presidents we must be amateur psychologists. But let's be good ones.

The phrase "amateur psychologist" has gained a slightly derogatory meaning, possibly because people in every walk of life consider themselves competent to practice psychology without knowledge or training. All too frequently we see unhappy examples of their less than professional competence.

But let's consider the amateur psychologist in another

ALFRED J. MARROW is Chairman of the Board, Harwood Manufacturing Corporation, New York City. He was formerly President of the firm.

frame of reference. Could any of us grow up successfully without learning to interpret the actions of others, without being sensitive to their needs and wants? And, especially in the process of becoming chief executives, haven't we had to be adept at predicting how people will react in a given situation? Haven't we had to learn to understand why they react as they do? These essential techniques of living form part of the basic subject matter of psychology, which aims to prove the validity of our common-sense assumptions and principles about people in their interactions with one another. The same techniques also form part of the daily life of the top executive.

Judging by the high divorce rate, the increase in intergroup conflict, and other evidences of our sick society, we might assume that the social sciences have not acquired any scientific understanding of why people behave the way they do. Judging, too, by the vast amount of interpersonal and intergroup conflict in industrial situations, we might assume that what company presidents know intuitively about people does not help them much in understanding people's behavior or lessening people's hostility. Yet, while the psychological sciences know little compared with the vast unknown, what they have already discovered is hardly being used at all and the public is scarcely aware of the substance of current research.

Large stockpiles of data about human beings have been assembled and analyzed but not yet put to use in answering the "why" of the day-to-day conflicts in and between groups. Ironically, the company president has to rely on his own intuitive assumptions about such matters as employees' frustrations, their levels of aspiration, their goals, how they look at company policies and practices, how they feel about the people they work for. The president's judgments in general are based on hit-or-miss assumptions that too often do not lead to valid predictions.

The claim is sometimes made that people could continue to cope with day-to-day problems of interpersonal relations even if all the scientific knowledge of human behavior were suddenly to disappear. It is stated that people would still know something about how to influence others, how to be sensitive to their needs; that people would still recognize when others were angry and know when they felt love or hate.

If this were true, it would merely point up the present failure to use what psychologists know about the conditions under which changes in human relations take place and the process by which these changes occur. Methods of measuring human capacities, of improving intergroup relations, of analyzing personality and character, and of interpreting perceptions and motivations are some of the techniques available—but not being used.

If presidents had a better understanding of these methods and a broader knowledge of human nature, especially their own, they could function at their best. This knowledge would then enable them to observe correctly how people affect each other at work and what this does to production and morale.

In his role as president, an individual is constantly

observing and evaluating the actions of others. But he is rarely aware that his reactions are founded on what he believes his subordinates are feeling, thinking, or perceiving.

As psychologist Hadley Cantril put it, "We are constantly seeing things not as they are but as we are. A man sees what he wants or expects to see in people." Thus the old adage "Seeing is believing" can be reversed and made even more accurate as "Believing is seeing." First an attitude is established; then evidence is selected to support the belief.

Hence people who manage others must acquire greater understanding of themselves and of others. The traditional pattern has been to increase the executive's skill in changing the ways in which other people behave toward one another. The answer to the question "Who is to be changed?" has been invariably "others"—not the president. Yet it is my belief that if the president is to be an ideal executive and earn the rating of "a good amateur psychologist," he must be ready to seek self-understanding before he tries to change others.

We find many people anxious to change others. The "others" may be the world, the government, the unions, or a man's colleagues, his children, or his wife. Rarely is it proposed that the president first seek to discover whether he needs to change the ways in which he behaves toward other people before he suggests that *they* ought to change.

I do not imply that all presidents need to change their perceptions of themselves and of others. But I do believe that they need to discover how accurately they perceive the way their subordinates see them, and whether they have been guilty of the common error of "looking at the other fellow from their own point of view." They need to know a lot more about the dependability of their judgments, of the intentions, motivations, and goals of their associates, and of their own frustration tolerance. They need to know whether their attitudes imply respect for the people who work for them or just a self-concern.

I have often asked groups of top executives to write answers to two questions: "What kind of person do you think you are?" and "What kind of person are you?" Their answers have then been compared with those of their subordinates to similar questions about these same top executives. The discrepancy between the president's self-image and his associates' perceptions of him makes misunderstandings between them inevitable.

It should not be concluded from these cases that it is always the president who is "blinded" to the feelings and emotions of the others. But this occurs oftener than we might expect because the president is less likely than any other member of the organization to hear criticism about his initiative, responsibility, emotional maturity, or ability to handle stress. Who among his subordinates is going to tell him?

Moreover, the way subordinates see the president is based, not just on the facts as they are, but on the facts as the subordinates see them in the light of their past experience and future expectations. Thus an employee who sees the president as a father figure, and who resents authority because of unhappy experience with his own father, will react critically to any act of the president. The president must learn to understand the meaning of such unfavorable attitudes and know how they should be treated.

Along with self-understanding, the president must acquire more understanding of the values that others bring to the work situation. For example, why do people work at all? What makes people work hard? Some answer that work as a virtue is a Christian concept. But it is the virtue of penance, not of fulfillment. It is a negative virtue: salvation from sin, not a positive wish to render life more abundant. The fact is that there are people to whom work is a pleasure and a fulfillment. They find embodied in their work the joys of sharing responsibility, participating in decision making, and receiving recognition for skill and good judgment. Such people want to participate.

But there are, of course, many kinds and degrees of participation, which can be grouped into three broad categories:

1. Low participation: When the employee is merely informed of a policy but is not encouraged to express an opinion about it.
2. Greater participation: When the reason for the policy is added to the statement of it.
3. Maximum participation: When the employee is

invited to make suggestions, clarify issues, face problems, and make decisions. Management's beliefs about the nature of man and what motivates him will determine whether employees are encouraged to participate.

If management believes that man instinctively hates work and avoids responsibility, it will introduce controls that will limit responsibility, initiative, and participation. On the other hand, if management believes that people seek a sense of achievement and want to be more than "hands," then it will give recognition for individual creativity, increase employee freedom in decision making, and reduce the degree of pressure and authority.

People enter industry after they have been molded and fashioned, educated and guided by parents and teachers. In recent years, this process has tended toward wider participation in family decisions by the younger members. In school and at home, youngsters are given greater freedom and encouraged to exercise more initiative. They get far fewer unexplained orders than they would have earlier in this century.

These are fundamental changes which create new expectations by youngsters entering the job market as to how they should be treated—expectations that affect their attitudes toward the company. And their attitudes often become hostile and negative because they find they are subject to controls that compel them to behave in a dependent and powerless manner. This passive behavior resembles the pattern of helplessness and dependency of early childhood which they were educated to leave behind them.

When employees who have gained a degree of maturity find they are forced to regress to earlier, unsatisfactory patterns of behavior, they react with inner resentment. It is as though they had finally grown up to be men and then were forced to act like boys again. Yet, in many companies, adults are made to behave like children because the management concept of their role requires it.

Childhood is distinguished from maturity in fundamental ways: by a development from dependence to independence (a change from helplessness to standing on one's own two feet); from immediate satisfaction of needs to long-range goals; from a short interest span to a long one; from being a subordinate member of the family to being an equal; from being powerless to having power; from having decisions made by others to making one's own decisions.

When adults come to our companies, what do they find? That in many ways they are compelled to return to an early stage of their development. They run athwart of three organizational features that tend to make them dependent, subordinate, compliant. These are:

1. The formal organization, the structure of the company. Whether centralized, divisionalized, or departmentalized, it limits what they can do and how much freedom they can express.
2. Their immediate supervisor. The kind of supervisor they have—whether he supervises closely or loosely,

whether he is directive or nondirective—will greatly influence the amount of freedom they have to function in their own areas.

3. Automatic controls—budgets, regulations, system policies. Budgets, for instance, may seem to some like a return to the limitations of a childhood allowance.

In order to obtain the advantages of "scientific" management in our companies, we have set up a great number of controls. As they work out, however, many of these neat business controls are brakes on the intelligence and responsibility of able men. They parallel the controls that the individual starting in industry finally grew away from at home—the rules of the company force him to act in a dependent and nonparticipant manner. And an emotionally mature adult reacts to dependency with hostility: Dependency does violence to his personality; it denies him some part, however small, in shaping the scheme of things he is in; he resents being placed in a position where no one wants to hear what he thinks or even wants him to think at all.

What can we do about this in our organizations? The question appears to pose a paradox: How can we follow accepted management principles and also accommodate the personality needs of our people?

As presidents, we may better understand these problems if we think of them in terms of our own personal reactions to government controls. Most businessmen object loudly to many of the controls imposed by government because they see their smothering effect in bureaucracy interfering with free initiative. But many presidents, while strongly denouncing government controls, tend to set up numerous bureaucratic controls in their own companies. Such controls are fundamentally born of distrust; they are marks of lack of faith in others.

Participation offers one answer to the apparent dilemma we face in applying sound management principles and at the same time accommodating the personality needs of employees.

Participation gives able people the kind of involvement in problem solving that encourages them to feel they are not being controlled to the point where their intelligence and responsibility are considered futile or worthless. In participation, we respect their ability and maturity by giving them freedom to discuss with each other, and with higher management, the problems which trouble them or the company. We seek their counsel on questions where they may have something to contribute.

Sometimes the recommendations people make will be followed, sometimes they won't—but in either case they have been treated as adults, they have had an opportunity to present their ideas. They will recognize that sometimes what we are seeking is their counsel, not their consent. In these situations they will recognize that the decision rests with others. With genuine participation we will have motivated people to work with us, instead of permitting their repressed hostility to get in the way of cooperation.

Making the participative approach compatible with the accepted principles of management is probably a matter of changing top management's attitude. It must become more receptive emotionally to shared leadership and broader opportunities in decision making at all levels. And this attitude change should start at the top, with the president.

Many presidents have seen the impressive results of sensitivity training in improving their subordinate executives' performance in interpersonal relations. In my judgment sensitivity training is essential to supplement even the most skilled common-sense understanding of the needs of others. Yet, thus far, few presidents have had the personal curiosity or courage to try it themselves.

Through sensitivity training, such as that offered at the National Training Laboratory at Bethel, Maine, or in AMA's Executive Action Course, the president can come to a much better understanding of himself and of how other people see him. For the president, the man whose work role deprives him most of a frank personality feedback from his associates, this confrontation with fellow group members who are not awed by his "back home" power and status can be especially valuable. And, rather than intellectually studying the principles of participation as stated by some outside source, he learns participation by living it emotionally in a series of group simulations. These sessions re-enact the realities of executive interaction without the considerations of status which ordinarily veil the president's perceptions of his employees' true feelings.

While sensitivity training should greatly facilitate interaction between the president and his staff—and, from this key interaction, ripple out to improve relations throughout the organization—the president will still carry many burdens which he cannot relieve by talking with his key executives. As the man with final responsibility and the full burden of leadership, he cannot communicate to anyone in the company most of his heaviest worries. In a sense the president is in "solitary," and in recent years social scientists have realized that a solitary man is an unnatural phenomenon and unable to function at his best.

To lighten the strain, the president may wish to retain a psychologically trained professional consultant on an available-when-needed basis. Such a consultant can help the president in several ways. He can act as a safety valve for the president to ease those tensions and anxieties which arise during periods of stress. He can help the president to understand his own feelings; he can assist the president to recognize when his decisions are based on fulfillment of his own personal needs rather than on company needs. And the professional consultant can provide a conduit for quickly and reliably passing into management practice the most recent advances and discoveries in the behavioral sciences. If the president is to be a good amateur psychologist, he should keep abreast of developments in the field and use such available techniques as self-appraisal, understanding of why employees resent paternalism, sensitivity training, and professional psychological consultation, since they can make him a more effective leader.

Fifty or so years ago, when being chief executive of a

company was a lot less complex and exacting a job than it is today, the company president could get his organizational feedback much more easily by personal contact than he can today.

Unfortunately, the "rugged individualist" tradition in American business leadership has made it seem a sign of weakness if the company president does not appear to have been born with almost inherited omniscience about himself and other people. Because of this tradition, many presidents feel a bit ashamed to be seen by their colleagues as being "in need of this kind of help" in handling the complex people problems associated with directing modern business.

However, just as he comfortably uses highly refined research and development concepts in solving product problems and as he simulates important decision problems with computers, the "forward-thinking president" will take advantage of self-appraisals, sensitivity training, and executive counseling in order to get better results in working through other people—as he must do to succeed in any technology.

The Burden of Ultimate Responsibility

1. *Loneliness Is Part of the Job*

Henry Schindall

On the night of August 26, 1776, in a tent in Brooklyn, General George Washington tossed and turned in his sleep. Several times his aides heard him moan and cry out. It was the eve of the Battle of Long Island.

In the morning, Washington's hastily gathered, untrained Continentals would face the powerful British army

Henry Schindall is President, Henry Schindall Associates, Inc., New York City.

and its Hessian mercenaries. The entire Continental army was at stake. It could be destroyed at one blow, and the patriot cause lost.

When morning came, Washington stepped out of his tent, cool and resplendent in his blue and buff uniform. He greeted his aides, mounted his white horse, and rode off to address his troops. Poised and unruffled, he answered their anxious, inquiring looks with a smile of confidence.

"Look at the General," one officer remarked to another. "You would think he was about to ride to hounds instead of against the British."

No one knows, of course, what Washington really thought or felt that morning. He could tell no one. He could turn to no one for support. He alone bore the ultimate responsibility. He was the man isolated at the top. He must have been a lonely figure.

In the same way, the president of a company is, in the deepest sense, a lonely man. I believe this sense of loneliness is the result of five characteristics that together make his job unique.

1. He alone has no peers.
2. He alone cannot lean on anyone for help in making a decision.
3. He alone cannot communicate freely.
4. He alone rarely gets information that is not slanted or colored.
5. He alone bears the burden of ultimate responsibility for the well-being of all.

The pinnacle at which the president lives and works sets him apart. He is alone in that little box at the top of the organization chart. Other managers have at least one peer and report to at least one superior and have at least one subordinate. The president alone has no superior, no equal—*only* subordinates. True, there is the board of directors. But the board is a multiperson, occasionally met group that rarely gets involved in the daily round of decision making.

The chief executive sets the tone and climate for the entire company. His personality, in large part, determines the company image. And, in turn, he is the prime target for praise or blame. Every executive and employee judges him not only as the president of the company but also as a public figure in the community. Like a political candidate, he is exposed constantly, on trial every moment.

The president stands by himself at the top of a human pyramid with no supporting arms to hold onto. ("The buck stops here," read a plaque on President Truman's desk.)

When an important decision has to be made, others in the company can look to higher authority to escape sole responsibility. The president has no such blessed relief. He makes the final decision. No one shares his burden. He is forced to rely on himself. It takes raw courage to say, "This is my decision. Right or wrong, I must stand by it." Stupid? Brilliant? Only time will tell.

Because his words and actions carry an enormous power to bolster or harm the organization and the people in it, the president must be especially careful when he communicates. And in communications we include that single word, that glance, that frown—even the way he dresses. Even the most trivial act can be misinterpreted.

The ability of the president's words and actions to influence others is an important tool of leadership. Used positively, the leader's charismatic powers can work miracles. Winston Churchill used them dramatically in his speeches to the British people during World War II when a hint of doubt might have panicked the British into submission. In a similar way, the president learns to watch his words and deeds: A firm handshake can reassure his vice president; a frown can start him wondering; a harsh word can send him job hunting. If the president innocently drops a word of doubt regarding a company project, that alone may doom it.

The president also learns to keep his own counsel. Rarely, if ever, does he openly express his doubts and fears. Says Ernest Henderson III, president, Sheraton Corporation: "About the only people the president can talk to are those he meets at outside meetings. And he cannot even talk to them in his own office."

Gregson Barker, president, Uarco, Inc., disagrees. "Anyone holding an executive position in any company is expected to treat matters in confidence and to reach decisions independently. A president is no different. He may at times have more problems, he may have to face alone some unpleasant situations, and he always has to accept responsibility for his company's results. But it seems he will do these things best if he simply goes about them as he does anything else—without trying to act differently than non-presidents."

Some presidents confide in their boards of directors. James A. Drain, president, Joy Manufacturing Co., feels this is one of the prime reasons for having a strong board. It is the solution he suggests to help overcome the chief executive's isolation.

Patrick L. McManus, group vice president, Worthington Corp., points out that the president possesses information concerning the future plans of his company (including the names of candidates for key positions) that cannot be shared with anyone but the board.

> This knowledge affects my day-to-day decisions and may make me appear arbitrary and unfair at times.
>
> The president has a unique and overriding responsibility for the success of the enterprise that transcends personal relationships and concern for personal popularity. The success of the enterprise is, at times, incompatible with the ambitions of individuals in the organization. Where other men enjoy popularity, the president must be satisfied with the respect of those who work for and with him.
>
> Nothing can be done to eliminate the president's isolation. But a staff that understands the president's job will appreciate the necessity for judgments which may seem arbitrary and occasionally unpopular.

The day after Henderson became president of Sheraton, a friend took him aside and said, "This is the last time you are going to hear the truth." Looking back, Henderson admits "there was a lot of truth in that remark."

The information that gets to the president is often colored, delayed, or changed in some fashion. It may be a natural distortion resulting from passing upward through several echelons. Or it may be deliberately revised along the way to make someone look good or to protect him from criticism. The president, as a result, is forced to dig beneath reported information.

Wheelock Bingham, when he was president of R. H. Macy & Co., stressed that a president must be careful about accepting a first opinion, especially if it is off the cuff. "Often you must query two or three people, sometimes five or six, to see the whole picture."

There may be very little slanting of information in some companies. In a company undergoing a power struggle between opposing cliques, however, the president's search for facts may be so blocked or sidetracked that he may become, to a degree, a captive of his top aides. They report only what they want him to hear. They carry out his policies as they wish and at their own pace. They are masters at slanting facts and making excuses.

The captive concept may imply weakness or inadequacy on the part of the president. This is not necessarily so. Even a strong president can fall into the trap.

Consider a president who is disturbed by constantly rising overhead costs and decides to do something about it. He calls together his operating committee to look into the problem. He goes around the table. Why are costs rising, the number of employees up, and profits falling? Each member, in turn, defends his own needs and gives excellent reasons for the rising budget in his own area. Increased costs, he says, are due to conditions beyond his control. He is struggling valiantly to hold them down, but he is under-staffed, working day and night. His solution: Other areas are fat, overstaffed, full of frills. Trim their budgets sharply. But his own area? Tight ship—much too tight, in fact.

So the meeting ends in a stalemate. The operating committee has presented the president with a solid front of locked shields against the threat of change.

Here's another example: A company decides to move its executive headquarters. Growth necessitates much larger quarters. President and board have agreed and specified objectives. Treasurer, controller, and vice president are par-ticipating in a profit-sharing plan; therefore, they are eager for net profits—immediate net profits. They object to the higher overhead expenses of larger quarters but are over-ruled. They bow to the president's wish.

The search job is given to a controller–vice president team. They are to find suitable quarters, negotiate, and follow through. Somehow, roadblocks develop. No office space is ever quite suitable; every promising deal falls through. A year goes by without a decision. The president is baffled.

Franklin D. Roosevelt once admitted he was com-pletely frustrated when he tried to get direct, plain answers from the Navy. It was like punching away at a featherbed, he said. Nothing ever happened except delays, excuses, evasion, inaction.

The company president can never be sure whether he really knows what is happening in his own company. Too often he cannot dig behind the facade that is presented for his inspection and approval. It is difficult to tell the apparent from the real. This uncertainty about the accuracy of his information increases his feeling of isolation.

The president is sometimes the last person to know what goes on in his own company. It takes quite a while for information to get up through channels to the top; facts can be blocked, revised, glossed over, changed before they reach his ears. To be sure, some presidents would disagree emphatically. Others admit it can happen—but only in other companies.

The president's job is, in many ways, a strange paradox. He is most sought after, most conferred with, most referred to. His life is usually filled to overflowing with other people. He is often an outgoing, gregarious fellow who deeply enjoys a rich and rewarding social life. Yet the president lives and works largely within himself, facing alone the burden of responsibility that he always carries with him.

Presidents may not always recognize their loneliness. Some object strenuously to the very idea. "Some presidents *are* lonely men," says Karl R. Bendetsen, president, Champion Papers, Inc., "but I do not agree that they need to be or should be. There are differences between the president's job and the jobs of others on the top management team, but they are only a matter of degree and centralization of responsibility."

Those who feel the uniqueness of the president's job maintain there is a marked "spotlight of responsibility clearly and completely on him," as Henry R. Roberts, president, Connecticut General Life Insurance Co., puts it. "The president's job often does not need to be as lonely as he makes it. Perhaps some feel that the authority and dignity of the office can be preserved only with a marked degree of aloofness."

"It is indeed a lonely job," says Dean T. Parker, president and general manager of A.G.E. Food Services, Inc., a division of Restaurant Associates Industries, "with more soul searching and frustration than any other job on the corporate ladder. Individual consultation with vice presidents and department heads is bound to create politics, if not handled correctly. A president has to encourage honest critique and 'bad news,' but he has to draw a fine line between what is good and important for the company and what seems to be opinionated backbiting. This of course does not make him exactly a 'pal,' and sometimes a subordinate who has been reprimanded repeatedly and asked to stay in his own bailiwick becomes quite uncommunicative. This obviously is the problem, but it looks as though presidents have to live with it. I have not been able to find an easy answer."

What can the president do to ease his sense of isolation? Wallace Johnson, president, Holiday Inns, has three ways of dealing with it:

> First, I am blessed with a wife who knows, understands, and is interested in my business. In fact, she holds an active position in many of our companies. I discuss everything with her, and her advice is always helpful.
>
> Second, . . . [the] chairman of the board and I work as a team, and I can always share my problems with him.
>
> Third, I have an assistant who works very closely with me. In some cases, I confide in him not so much to get his advice, but just to be able to tell my problems to someone.

For a final word on the subject, here are the thoughts of Conrad N. Hilton, chairman of the board, Hilton Hotels Corporation:

> I concur that a company president is a lonely man, but if he has adequate inner resources, he also is a most fortunate man.
>
> The isolation which a company president at times experiences is far outweighed by the rewards of the position. He is like a symphony conductor; he expresses his personality by drawing together diverse elements and individual skills to create a unified work. Indeed, few occupations present the opportunities for such fulfillment. If, in his pursuit of excellence, he lets his watchwords be honesty, trust, and mutual confidence, he will

develop meaningful human relationships with his business associates.

While a company president must inevitably trust his own judgment, he cannot succumb to the arrogant temptation to feel that he needs no one.

He must look within and above himself to that unlimited source of soul-sustenance—God. The company president who completely yields to God's authority will find a fountain of strength that will carry him through even the most demanding confrontations with difficult decisions.

2. *A President Doesn't Have to Be Lonely*

Lawrence P. White

THERE's a notion that the president automatically becomes isolated from the rest of the people in his company. His people tend to hold him and his office in awe, the reasoning goes, and he responds by further withdrawing.

I'm sure this happens, but I don't believe it happens automatically. Fact is, it doesn't have to happen at all. Here's my experience.

I came to The Fredericks Company in 1959 as the new president. Not only was the job new to me, but so were the people. This was true of not only the people in the com-

LAWRENCE P. WHITE is President, The Fredericks Company, Huntingdon Valley, Pennsylvania.

pany but its customers and suppliers, too. Yet it wasn't long before I felt as much at home as I was in the company I had worked for the previous 13 years.

This didn't surprise me. A man carries his skills and talents with him into the new job as president—if he has them to begin with. The job doesn't change the man. More likely, it dramatically brings out his strengths and weaknesses. It doesn't separate him from his associates. A competent and confident chief executive draws people to him.

The man who is isolated at the top probably took the first step toward loneliness by withdrawing from his staff. The gap he created gets wider as his people draw back in response. The problem is created by the man, not the job.

When I joined the Navy, I saw the world of difference between men. On an aircraft carrier in the Pacific during the War, we had four different commanding officers in two years. Only one was really lonely, and he set himself apart from his officers and crew. His aloof bearing guaranteed his isolation.

At sea during wartime, a captain is, of course, confined to the bridge. But I remember well how one of our captains, Austin K. Doyle (later vice admiral), mingled with the officers and men by having them visit him on the bridge or in his main cabin when the ship was at anchor.

It is a big change for an officer to move from the friendly company of the wardroom to the private quarters of the commanding officer. His primary responsibility now is to command; his secondary responsibility is morale. Captain Doyle met his responsibilities by bringing out the best in his people, by showing them that he was interested in their job performance.

This applied to enlisted men as well as officers. Because he could not leave the bridge while at sea, Captain Doyle would personally congratulate those who had done outstanding jobs by asking them to come to see him. They quickly got the message that the captain appreciated their good work.

Captain Doyle communicated with his men individually and in groups, in face-to-face discussions and over the loudspeaker. He kept the crew abreast of things that had happened or were expected to happen. It wasn't long after he reported on board that the mess cooks confirmed what everybody suspected: We had a fine skipper. And, as anybody who has served in the Navy knows, cooks are right in on the dope.

A company president has similar responsibilities for leadership and morale. It seems to me that a president who fully realizes the importance of morale in his company will naturally try to draw his employees closer to him through the various means of communication at his disposal.

Like the captain who runs a happy ship by keeping the channels of communication open, I maintain an open-door policy at all times. I want my employees at every echelon to feel that they can stop in and visit with me.

Nearly all of us have had annoying experiences with overprotective secretaries who have prevented us from seeing our company president or the president of some other company. The well-meaning individual sitting in front of a closed door marked "PRESIDENT" may not be guarding his busy schedule so much as his secret wish to avoid the many difficult decisions a president has to make. Maybe he never wanted to become president in the first place, but was forced into the office by circumstances. Though he may have been groomed since his youth to take over a small family business, he may be unqualified by training or temperament. Size of company or type of ownership is not, of course, the critical factor. It's still the man.

Most men who get to be president have proved their ability to delegate, to lead men, to bring out the best in people and develop their skills, to make decisions and to distinguish information that is reliable and complete from information that is twisted and tainted. Training and intuition have taught them to anticipate the right answers to their questions. Subordinates, in turn, have learned they cannot slip them shoddy information and expect to get away with it.

Such a man does not need an overprotective secretary. He is available to people who want to see him and to those who want to call him on the telephone. At times, he answers his own phone so that he can easily be reached by his company's important customers and suppliers and by those who report directly to him. It is a simple matter to provide the switchboard operator with a list of persons who should have a straight-through line to the president.

I keep a direct line of communication open not only to my closest associates but to managers as far down as the foreman level. For example, we hold informal meetings with foremen. After the first meeting or two, it didn't take long for them to tell us about problems we never expected or suspected. This is part of the important feedback that puts me and my top executives in a better position to help people do a better job—a major responsibility of every president.

Meeting this responsibility is the most pleasant part of my job. I consider myself lucky to be a manufacturer because it gives me the daily opportunity to go through the plant and talk with the employees about business or personal interests or just to share a good laugh.

On my first plant tour the day I joined the company, I asked the personnel manager to introduce me to the employees. His standard introduction went something like this: "This is our new president. We are all happy to have him with us." One woman's reply was to the effect that she would make up her own mind in due course. Right then and there I made up my mind that I would get to know the people who worked in the company.

Now I try to meet every new employee the first day he or she starts work. It's the swiftest way I know to assure an employee that his individual efforts are important—and appreciated. And it's the surest way to maintain high morale.

The personnel manager once summed it up for me by citing a familiar management principle. It's an old saying, but it holds true: "Morale doesn't well up from the bottom, it trickles down from the top."

Stop Protecting Yourself
from Mistakes

An interview with Robert C. Townsend

M̲r̲. T̲o̲w̲n̲s̲e̲n̲d̲, *do you think most chief executives are setting the proper working climate for their organizations?*

Definitely not. By and large, top management today is too fat. Most of our big companies started and grew when their chief executives were lean and hungry. Today, they are no longer lean and hungry.

While every company pays lip service to the claim that leadership is vital, few of them do anything to implement the idea. In fact, leadership usually consists of defending

R̲o̲b̲e̲r̲t̲ C. T̲o̲w̲n̲s̲e̲n̲d̲, since January 2, 1969, has been Director and Chairman of the Executive Committee of CRM Inc., Del Mar, California. Mr. Townsend was Chairman of the Board, Avis, Inc.

the status quo. Top managements in American companies today usually breathe a huge sigh of relief at having joined the inner circle; then they spend the rest of their time defending that inner circle and preventing the ideas of others from getting a proper hearing.

Chief executives often set up status walls between themselves and the rest of the company. As a result, they are overprotected from their own mistakes. This interest in being protected and avoiding responsibility and mistakes soon spreads throughout the company.

How can a chief executive break out from behind his wall of protection?

The first thing is to make a realistic self-appraisal of your own performance. Most chief executives I know never do this. If they did, they would learn a lot about their own jobs and gain a new insight into how to lead their executives. It would give them a new idea about the importance of making mistakes and the valuable lessons you can learn from them.

The point is that there is nothing wrong with making mistakes. But chief executives are a funny group. Somewhere along the line they become infallible. By definition, they don't make mistakes; so they become less tolerant of mistakes in their subordinates. The result is that people all down the line start spending too much of their time covering up mistakes when they should be facing up to them and doing something about them, such as getting help from the chief executive if necessary.

My policy is to follow the rule of errors: If a man has

the responsibility for a result, he should be permitted to make the normal errors in decisions necessary to achieve that result. The fact is, if he is not making plenty of mistakes, he probably isn't making enough decisions or he isn't making them fast enough.

Isn't it human nature to cover up mistakes?

Don't misunderstand me. You don't have to nail everyone's mistakes on the bulletin board. This is one of the commonest errors in business today. When a mistake is identified as a mistake, the head of the company or the head of the department starts a search to find out who made it. This tends to drive mistakes underground and to slow down decision making.

Do you believe in consultants to help the chief executive make difficult corporate decisions?

No. Consultants make their living by protecting chief executives from problems and saving them from having to make difficult decisions where they might make mistakes. This isn't true of all of them, of course, but it is true of many.

There are two easy ways out for a chief executive when he runs into a difficult decision. One is to appoint a committee to study the problem and recommend a solution. Committees are more likely to make a mistake than an individual, however, because they try to take the path of least resistance, which is very frequently wrong. Or they try to play it safe, and the safe way also has a high chance of being wrong.

The chief executive often appoints a committee so he can share the blame with it if things go wrong. I don't accept this kind of protection. There are no management committees where I am in charge; so I don't waste anybody's time in committee meetings.

The other easy way to avoid making a difficult decision is, as you say, to hire a consultant to make it for you. The trouble is, consultants are even more likely to make mistakes than a committee, because they start with little or no knowledge of the business or of the people in the company.

These two means of making the chief executive's life easier and, in turn, keeping the corporate atmosphere calm should be avoided. He must come to grips with the problem himself, ask for advice from within the company, and then make the decision. But, more important, *he* must make the decision.

What about the board of directors?

The board, in my opinion, has one overriding function —to keep the chief executive on the payroll or fire him. Everything else the board does is minor compared to this. Naturally, the directors should offer him the benefit of their experience, advise and consult with him, review his version of the company's performance with the regular reports of financial data issued to them, and, in general, try to be helpful.

Directors should look to the chief executive to organize and motivate the company. When they are dissatisfied with the results, their remedy is to fire him—and they should feel free to exercise that right.

Are companies getting the best possible performance from their executives?

Most companies are using their human resources poorly. You can break down the reasons for this into two categories. First, top management is not using enough carrots or is using the carrots improperly. Second, many chief executives prevent their people from trying hard and working hard.

I have strong feelings on the matter of executive compensation. After all, money is the single most important motivation. Most chief executives I know don't really want a whole lot of people in their company to make more money. They don't have a passion to see executives who make $15,000 improve their usefulness to the point where they can make $30,000. They would rather keep salaries in strict categories.

The result is that compensation systems are run very beautifully and without any chaos at all—by the personnel department. They're designed to keep the chief executive's life calm and to keep compensation problems out of his office. This tends to homogenize everybody. It stabilizes and frustrates. It undercompensates the outstanding person and overcompensates the poor performers. Stars tend to leave, and dullards spend their limited talents trying to stay on the payroll.

Do you believe in wide variations in income for executives doing pretty much the same jobs? Are you personally involved in compensation decisions?

119

The way you phrased the question means you don't really understand it.

There are two parts to any sound executive "income" system. First is base pay. That's what the job is worth compared to competing jobs in other similar companies in the area.

Once a year the top 30 or so of us at Avis would sit down in one room and go over the base pay of all the people in the room and all the people who reported to us to make sure the pay was fair. (Jobs change all the time, and in any given year some will have grown more critical. Some will be less critical.) Done en masse, this saves time and encourages justice. In individual sessions some people will be better promoters of themselves and their people than others. In one big session like this the inequities stand out and are rectified.

Two weeks later, the same group would meet again to judge performance for the past year. We tried to keep it simple. Each man or woman who made over $7,500 a year or who managed people (supervisor of a key-punch gang, for example) was eligible. Each was given one of three ratings by his boss: outstanding, satisfactory, or unsatisfactory. Satisfactory got $1X$ percent of base salary, outstanding got $2X$ percent of base salary, and unsatisfactory got nothing. The pool available was known: 15 percent of pretax profits less formula bonuses (for example, the manager of Peoria Rent-a-Car and his key people would get 3 percent of Peoria's profits). The treasurer then would take all the base salaries and all the $1X$'s and $2X$'s and calculate X. The first year it was zero because the company lost money. The second year it was 15 percent, the third year 35 percent, and the fourth year 55 percent.

Also, it's important that each of the 30 of us handed a check (or no check) to each man who reported to us and told him how we had rated him for the past year. If you have no check for a man, you have his full attention when you tell him why.

Who rated your performance? Is the chief executive's total compensation a problem?

I did. But the board of directors reviewed and approved. My rating varied between unsatisfactory (no check) and satisfactory. I never made the outstanding list.

The top man's compensation *can* become a problem, especially when the company becomes successful. Chief executives often receive pay and benefits 'way out of proportion to their contributions. The board of directors tends to overvalue the chief executive's importance because he is the man the members talk to. Everything that goes right with the company they attribute to him.

But overcompensation of the chief executive leads to an infallibility complex. Or it leads to fear of being wrong and tends to make him play it safe. Sometimes it makes him want to contribute his so-called magic touch to everything, and this slows down the whole organization. And of course overcompensation of the chief executive means others are relatively underpaid, and any lack of justice is unhealthy.

Did anyone in Avis make more than you as a result of your incentive plan?

Yes—sometimes. There is a myth that the chief executive has to be paid more than anybody else. I think it's ridiculous.

I regard the chief executive's function as being like that of Vince Lombardi, formerly coach of the Green Bay Packers and now with the Washington Redskins. And I see no reason why the coach should be paid more than the Paul Hornungs or Bart Starrs who do the scoring on the field.

Is it true that you believe job descriptions have a negative effect in motivating subordinates?

Sure, giving people a formally written job description tends to demean them. When you describe in clumsy prose what they regard as an exciting job, it takes all the fun out of it.

Chances are that in sitting down with an executive to write his job description, I may—merely by shrugging a shoulder or lifting an eyebrow—convey the idea that I give little importance to something he regards as critical. The result is that his enthusiasm for working for me will begin to sag. Later on, when his job has changed in nature, he may say to himself, "I'm not even working in the area of this job description. Should I go back and get it rewritten? Good Lord, I don't want to sit down with that fink again."

Another trouble is that poor performers tend to hide behind a job description. You can walk through a company and almost smell that it has job descriptions because it's quiet and there is absolutely no chaos, no action.

What about organization charts?

The minute you draw a box around a man's name, you limit him—in his own mind at least—to whatever is written in that box. If he is a poor performer, he ignores every other task or responsibility because he figures that it isn't his concern. The only good thing about charts is that they tell you where the troubles are. Just look for the dotted lines— they'll tell you what people, functions, and divisions are not working effectively.

Did Avis have any organization charts?

Yes, I'm afraid we did. We had two charts, one for each operating division. But I didn't encourage their publication because I consider such charts offensive.

I'll give you an example of what I mean. The average chart is a beautiful thing. Sometimes people write on it that the level of the boxes has no relationship to rank. They've eliminated that problem—or so they think. But often they go to great lengths to arrange the boxes with a great regard for the niceties of status. I hate this. By putting a man a little below where he thinks he belongs on a sheet of paper, you reduce his enthusiasm; and a little bit of life goes out of the job and the company, too.

Again, the organization chart is often designed and used to settle questions of responsibility and authority, and to make the chief executive's life and everyone else's a little more peaceful. But I don't think that's a suitable objective. His job shouldn't be peaceful.

Do you believe in promoting people from within?

Most American firms proclaim that promoting from within, whenever possible, is their practice. But when a key job comes up they usually look outside. Nobody inside the company looks as good to his boss as the outside person does. This unfortunate attitude not only stultifies the growth of individuals within a company, it also compels younger executives to change jobs to get the advancement they deserve.

Let's take a sensitive position, like that of sales manager. If I had to fill it, I would start with the company's outstanding performers last year—in any field, whether it was related to sales or not—and see if any one of them could be promoted to the job. Of course, you've got to interview him and make sure he is ambitious and hungry and intelligent, and regards the job as a challenge and opportunity.

The fact that he doesn't know anything about sales management is an asset. He already knows the basic nature of the company, and he has the respect of his comrades going for him. In a service organization, he's got to be good at dealing with people; and, if he wasn't sales-minded, he probably wouldn't have gotten as far as he has in the company. In two years he will have opened a fantastic amount of water between himself and a fellow hired from the outside.

My rule of thumb is this: If a man looks to be 50 percent of what you want for the job and he is an outstanding performer in any field in the company, it's almost certain that he'll grow the other 50 percent in a remarkably short time.

You believe strongly in exposing executives to problems and letting them sink or swim. How have you increased your own personal exposure?

I came to the conclusion a while back that top executives are protected by their secretaries from worthwhile contacts with people inside and outside the company. I decided at Avis that my efficiency would rise if I got rid of mine, which I did. My efficiency rose quite a bit as a result. Instead of a personal secretary, I called on any one of 14 girls in a special group called staff services.

These girls were energetic and skillful. They believed that it's more fun—and the day goes quicker—if you work hard instead of sitting at your desk and reading novels. The trouble in most companies is that the secretaries of some top executives are underemployed. Their days just drag along, and they are bored to tears. As a result, they demoralize the busy ones.

This staff service group at Avis was a high-morale outfit. They knew that if they worked hard they could move ahead. A former head of the group, by the way, graduated to become supervisor of the customer service department.

A great thing happened when the staff service group replaced my secretary—my files disappeared. I looked through all the files and threw out everything I could not keep in my desk.

Another thing: I had to dial my own telephone calls, and I got them much faster than I used to. I used to buzz my secretary to make a call for me and then remember that I had just sent her on an errand. So I'd just sit there and chew my nails until she got back.

Chances are, she picked that time to stop and pass the time of day with a few office friends. Executives should try calling their own offices sometimes. They'll see how often their secretaries are out gassing with the girls.

Did you handle all your own telephone calls?

I had three rules for the switchboard. One, it put through any Avis employee anywhere in the country who called and said, "I want to talk to Mr. Townsend." Two, any customer who said, "I have a complaint and I want to speak to the top man," came right through. Three, any reporter or analyst from a responsible organization also got right through to me.

This last rule is an important one. Too often the chief executive sets up a group called public relations, and all it does is destroy his relations with the public by protecting him *from* the public. Anyone who is devoted to protecting the chief executive is probably also protecting him from doing his job right.

The truth is, too many top executives are protected from outside calls.

What happened when you had a confidential matter to handle or when you went on a business trip?

I think secrecy is greatly overrated in business. As a result, communication is greatly undermined. Ninety percent of the matters the chief executive regards as highly confidential deal with his own expense account or personal affairs. Having a confidential secretary encourages him to be profligate with company funds. I'd just as soon post my expense account on the company bulletin board.

As to needing a personal secretary to cover your office when you go on trips, let me give you two examples. I went away for a three-week vacation one January. I told the staff services people that when I came back I didn't want one scrap of paper waiting on my desk. I didn't want a single letter. I didn't want anything. I was going to start off as though I'd never been away.

I told the group to give every letter to someone in the organization. If in doubt, they were to throw it away because, if it were important, people would write again. There wasn't a scrap of paper on my desk when I came back.

One of our executives had a very efficient secretary who acted as an assistant. When *he* came back after three weeks, his desk was piled two feet high with things to do. That's because an assistant or executive secretary can't act for an executive in his absence. What he or she can do— and often does—is prevent anyone else from handling the problems.

What about the myth that some chief executives have more work than they can handle?

It's not a myth, but it doesn't have to be true, either. If a chief executive is so harried and overworked, chances are he is paid so much that he has come to the conclusion that he is indispensable. He insists on reviewing in advance everything that is going to be done. As a result, the company's decision making grinds along at 20 percent of optimum.

The idea of delegation of authority is typical. Everyone says it's great, but in the average American company the chief executive just pays lip service to the principle. He's trying to protect himself from other people's errors, but the result is often just the reverse of what he wants—less efficient operations and lower profits.

To summarize, what can a chief executive do to free himself from the overprotective attitude that shields him and his subordinates from making decisions?

First, he should increase his respect for the human beings that work for him. He should assume that there are going to be mistakes made below in the line, but he should not be afraid of mistakes. As he frees up the company and allows people to make decisions—and mistakes—he will see outstanding performers appear all over the lot. Then he should be sure that they are outstandingly compensated for their efforts.

If somebody from outer space looked down and saw a chief executive doing what I have urged here, he would say: "Good Lord, that's just common sense. There's nothing unusual about that." But, if he saw what is going on in the average company today, he would be appalled.

He Charts His Course
on the Seven C's

H. H. Scott

Our high-fidelity stereo-component business has grown by 20,000 percent since I founded the company some 20-odd years ago. But there have been some dark moments along the way.

Several years ago, for example, our tuners and tuner-amplifiers featured rotary dials instead of the conventional linear "slide rule" dials. It looked as though we had a real advantage over competition: Our rotary dials were cheaper to make, easier to operate, and more distinctively styled. I learned the hard way that prospective customers, not being

H. H. Scott is President, H. H. Scott, Inc., Maynard, Massachusetts.

technically oriented, were scared off by the rotary dial's "instrument" look. A major competitor with a technically inferior product outsold us for better than a year. There was nothing to do but convert to the familiar sliding dial and profit from a lesson in the danger of seemingly good concepts that do not take into account the realities of the marketplace.

I learned to watch for this pitfall, and many others, during two decades in a business experiencing explosive growth, fierce competition, constant technical change, and —despite our failure to sell round dials in a still square market—shifting tastes by consumers. Our successes and failures during this challenging period have taught me that the man at the helm of a growing business in a competitive industry has to be able to see the rocks and reefs ahead. And he must stay on course despite wind and fog. The stormier the seas, the greater the challenge—and the more skillful the skippers who survive.

The skills and knowledge I've acquired along the way are summed up in this mnemonic device that charts the course for smooth sailing on the seven C's of the business world:

The Concept of Concentration on Choosing a Crew to whom you Communicate your Commitment to Change.

First, *Concept.* Right or wrong, the chief executive's concepts of the future are the most important elements in building a business. Intangible concepts largely determine what kind of business we build and how we build it. In business, where tangibles such as people, plant, and product are important, it may seem unrealistic to put primary emphasis on concept. But, if anything, we should increase this emphasis. The clarity of concepts in top management largely decides what tangible forms will be created.

Since human thinking and action are goal-directed, the greater the clarity of concept, the more effective the ensuing action.

My New England background has conditioned my concepts with a stamp of prudence, ingenuity, and demanding standards. When our business was new, we had dreams of building superior new products that would win us recognition and lead to growth. We held to the concept that a business could make important contributions to the community. We also believed that while our resources were limited, if we had to make do, we could. Whereas, if we borrowed heavily, we could find some way to spend the money.

We now have a showplace plant. We did much of the design and planning ourselves, saving substantially on construction costs. Here was our prudence concept. While we have won many awards for technical and marketing innovations, I am proudest of the award from the President's Committee on Employment of the Physically Handicapped. Here was our concept of community responsibility.

One of our key concepts for coping with our present and creating our future is *Concentration*. My original intent in going into the stereo business was to concentrate on the manufacture of professional engineering-laboratory instruments. Our 210-A amplifier, introduced in 1946, was designed as a vehicle for using the dynamic noise suppressor patents which had aroused much excitement.

As it turned out, our 210-A proved to be the first modern commercial high-fidelity component amplifier. When component markets grew faster and showed more opportunity than did acoustic-measuring instruments, we altered our sights and concentrated most of our time, thought, and company resources on amplifiers.

Only later did we start making tuners, and then we concentrated on technical innovations until we also were the principal factor in tuners. Basically, we focused our efforts in an opportunity area until we mastered it.

This principle of concentration is also useful in allocating executive time. Too often, insistent day-to-day crises intrude, and the all-important future is left to fend for itself—at great peril. I find I must discipline myself to reserve time to think about the future, and no time is put to better use.

Choosing, or decision making, is another critical function of command. It takes much effort and information even to crystallize complex situations into alternatives ready for choice. Seldom are enough facts available to make the right choice obvious. Missing pieces have to be filled in by the commander, who must rely on experience, judgment, or just intuition.

A logical approach to information gathering and synthesis is important. But, unfortunately, formal logic breaks down when problems of people or timing are involved, and these are really the most difficult areas of choice.

A significant part of choosing is simply to select that point at which to use intuitive approaches. It is here that success or failure is largely determined. Here systematic information synthesis must bow to the president's concepts. Does he maintain, and preferably accelerate, the momentum of his organization's forward thrust? At which point are new injections of people, product, or plant required to sustain the company's tempo? I know of no way to develop this sense of timing and tempo other than through experience—learning from unavoidable mistakes. Here is the point at which the art of business takes over from the science of business.

Part of this art is attracting and choosing the chief executive's *Crew*. In this people-picking process, even the most careful interviewing and background checks can't eliminate all mistakes. But as important as picking good people is placing them in areas of their greatest strengths, interests, and, hence, potential. By concentrating their efforts in these areas, we expect a return ten times greater than if we nagged them to correct all their weaknesses.

Building a crew is like building a New England stone wall. Where a big rectangular rock is needed, don't use 30 pebbles. Where a small triangular stone is needed, search through your pile for one of the right size; don't chip it off a larger rock.

We try to build teams where one executive's strength

neutralizes and supplements another's weakness. By using this synergistic process, we make 1 and 1 equal 11. Where one manager is analytical, factual, and cautious, he needs the inspiration of another manager's dynamism and feel for intangibles of people and market. Yet the former adds prudence and order. Thus all our people use themselves at close to fullest potential and gain that satisfaction from that achievement which is a vital factor in growth.

We encourage people to take risks despite conceivable costs in errors. If they are not allowed to fail, they won't learn how to make better choices in the future. This can soon create a climate of frustration and fear which freezes people into rigid patterns. Forward thrust dies. No one sticks his neck out. The weaker become timeservers, the stronger leave, and bureaucracy results.

Again, art enters—because, if you choose strong people, they can be mighty difficult at times. You have to find that elusive dividing line between freedom and frustration, conveying to your crew your own concepts of capitalizing on opportunity and correcting error.

The commander's prime tool here is his capacity to *Communicate*. Through words, we reach others—crew, customer, community. But effective communication is complex, involving concepts such as transmission, reception, and semantics.

Most conflicts I encounter are based on some sort of misunderstanding. To achieve understanding, chaotic sense impressions must be converted into coherent and intelligible relationships. Most flaws in this process occur because the parties are more interested in transmitting their own messages than in hearing and comprehending what the other party has to say. An exchange of messages—whether in memo or speech—is not a real exchange of meaning unless there is mutual feedback.

People respond to people, things, and ideas—in that order. Ideas or things are best communicated in terms of people, particularly that person most important to the listener—himself. So the magic key to capturing attention is to answer the other fellow's unstated question: "What's in it for me, now?"

Messages are external; meanings are internal. Meanings are found in a person's reactions to messages—reactions colored by the listener's emotions, personality, experience, and needs. Here is ample chance for failure in communicating. If the listener hasn't heard or understood, the speaker hasn't communicated. If the listener is your customer, you have to make sure you get through—or you may lose him.

Quality control on our stereo products is detailed and rigid, yet we do get customer complaints. We find that misuse by the customer is often at fault, not the equipment. The loudspeakers are not hooked up correctly, the antenna is inadequate, some of the switches or adjustments are in the wrong position, or the tuner isn't tuned to the right frequency. The customer has ignored instructions, to his and our disadvantage.

Moreover, the trend toward international operations is putting greater emphasis on the art of communication. Since we set up our international division, our chief problems have been caused, not by different foreign languages, but by different internal languages such as "salesese" and "engineeringese."

"The successful men usually are those who have talked their way upward," Bruce Barton once observed. This may be true, but the critical weakness in communication is still listening. Most people transmit at great rates, skillfully or sloppily. Too often, however, their receivers are turned off. And, unless you listen not just to the words people speak but also to what they mean, you can miss valuable information in conception, concentration, and choosing.

One of my most important techniques in motivating my crew is to show interest in the other man's position. Understanding often involves much probing and give-and-take of facts. Receptivity to any effort to impart meaning is essential. Whether or not I agree with what is said, I listen until I have its meaning. The more I dislike what I hear, the more effort I make to suspend judgment.

A rule of thumb at conferences is to hear the other fellow out before you try to counter his position. In too many discussions, the listener doesn't attempt to winnow out the meaning of a message; he simply marshals his rebuttals while waiting for the chance to pounce, even before the speaker has finished. Too often, the result is a swapping of many messages but little meaning. Solutions, then, are superficial, coping only with symptoms.

Almost always, I find a free two-way exchange far easier if I listen with a third ear for what people mean—not just to what their words seem to say. Discussion plays an essential part in the ordering of information needed to achieve a full grasp of meaning. But such understanding is only the takeoff point from which individuals make that leap of faith and commitment represented by decision.

Commitment, the will to win, is closely allied to standards. The old army answer, "No excuse, sir!" merits more attention than it gets in these days of misapplied wishy-washy human relations. Once a choice has been made and the organization is committed, it becomes vital to brook no slacking-off. The best human relations is to insist on superior performance from your people. This forces them to learn and to grow by coping with challenge, and it develops in them a pride of achievement.

When we introduced the first FM-stereo multiplex tuner, for example, we did so with trepidation. At the urging of our sales department, we had asked engineering to design equipment for the four multiplex systems we thought most likely to be approved by FCC. Engineering claimed this was utterly impossible, but we insisted. We had committed ourselves publicly to being first, and the engineers just had to come through. And as so often happens, once this commitment was communicated to them, they somehow were able to meet it. Result: We scored a clear-cut technical beat over the rest of the industry. In fact, time-switching multiplex, one of our contributions to the art, has become standard in the hi-fi audio industry.

People do not learn, grow, or change unless it hurts them worse to stay the way they are. I am willing to cause suffering if that appears to be the best course. This can make me unpopular, but it also makes me respected. The higher the standards of performance, the more people are encouraged to reach for their full potential. In enforcing standards, example is the best tool. In crises, most people are only too glad to follow the man who knows where he's going. The man who meets conflict with confidence and even zest provides a dynamic model for the people in his organization.

This brings us to the last C. *Change* has never been more rapid than now, when nine out of ten scientists who have ever lived are still alive and technical knowledge doubles every ten years. Past standards seem obsolete. We can either cause our competition to adapt to changes we create or we may be forced to adapt to theirs.

Change can hurt. It causes disruption which invariably means resistance. But in the long run it hurts worse to resist change than to create it. As Joseph Schumpeter, the late Harvard economist, pointed out: "Profit results from the innovator's advantage and therefore disappears when the innovation becomes routine."

This truth has certainly been proved again and again. I feel proud when I look back at some of the changes within our industry caused by our innovations. Yet I recall only too well our fears and doubts when we launched the first stereo amplifier, our 299. It was new, expensive—and a shot in the dark. But it hit the mark. That year we sold five times our most optimistic forecast on the 299's.

Introduction of the first FM-stereo multiplex tuner also meant painful disruption of the status quo, plus a high degree of risk in terms of committing our organization's most critical resources. Not introducing it, however, would have been a greater risk.

The future is largely unknowable, but since it is not yet upon us it is also malleable. With enough imagination and momentum, with good concepts, concentration of resources, choice of crew, and commitment, the future can be created on our own terms. Change can be an ally rather than an enemy. Obviously, the best that can be hoped for is a good batting average. After all, when Ted Williams batted .406 he was still out six out of ten. I try to minimize the risk of creating change by always having enough irons in the fire. If an unforeseen crisis creeps up, one or more irons may be hot enough to use.

Command can be a lonely state, beset by risk and uncertainty. To meet inevitable blows, flexibility is the answer. A rigid commander, like a rigid organization, eventually cracks. The essence of growth, change, health, and maturity is an open, receptive, flexible approach to coping with problems of reality. A closed mind and rigid patterns based on past problems and solutions seem more soothing, but actually they are invitations to disaster.

So we come back full-circle to concepts. Perhaps the best reason for navigating the seven C's is that only through this process can the skipper himself learn and grow. He bounces back from adversity and usually finds some way to turn a crisis into an opportunity. He has a vast advantage over less daring competitors because he is willing to create his own future—and that's where the fun is.

How I Got Hooked
on Objectives

Berkley W. Bedell

I STARTED my company when I was 15 years old, but I
didn't really learn how to run it until I was 40. That was
1961, the year I discovered that a company exists for a
purpose.

I founded Berkley and Company when I was a high
school sophomore. My specialty was making fishing flies
and my workshop the bedroom of the family's frame house
in Spirit Lake, Iowa. A $50 investment from a newspaper
route bought $30 worth of hooks and feathers and a $20 ad

BERKLEY W. BEDELL is President, Berkley and Company, Inc., Spirit
Lake, Iowa.

in an outdoor magazine. Summer sales netted $100. That was 1937.

Backed by a $1,000 family fund, I went into business full-time upon graduation from high school in 1939. My plan was to make a good-quality fishing leader out of wire instead of woven linen (the usual material at the time) and to undersell the big companies. Without being sure that I could do it, I set prices 10 percent below competition and drove 3,000 miles through the Midwest picking up $10,000 in orders.

By sheer luck, I walked into a machine shop in South Bend, Indiana, that was making wire-leader soldering rigs for major fishing-tackle manufacturers. I bought a rig and headed home, ready to take on the big competition. I purchased materials with a bank loan and undertook my first plant expansion—I took over a small storeroom in the back of the house.

By 1942, the year I locked the company doors and went off to war, the main production area was a partitioned-off section of the Masonic hall. There were also piecework subsidiaries in cellars and unused corners of homes throughout the community. When we went back into production in 1945, a pent-up postwar demand made it easy to double sales and profits every year for the next several years. We built a three-story plant and then started looking for lofts and garages to convert into additional production space. Berkley and Company was soon operating seven "plants" in Spirit Lake (pop. 2,800).

In 1960, a community development corporation helped raise $100,000 toward a new $350,000 plant. A loan from the Small Business Administration made up the difference. In 1961, we moved our 250 employees and all the equipment into the plant. We were under one roof for the first time.

That summer I sat at a round table with other presidents and discovered that for 24 years I had been running the company pretty much without objectives or purpose—either corporate or personal. The other chief executives talked about goals and management principles: what they were trying to do and how they were going about it. I listened. "Every business should exist for a purpose. Profit by itself is not enough," a speaker said. I agreed. "The first step in professional management is to write out objectives," he said. "If they aren't written out, you don't have them."

I asked myself, "Berk, what are your objectives? Why are you running the company?" I didn't know.

I was 40 years old, financially secure, the chief executive of a growing, prosperous company. I worked long, hard hours, but my family lived comfortably, my employees had steady, good-paying jobs, and the community had a hometown business to be proud of. Judged by most people's standards, I was a success. But what about *my* standards? What had I set out to achieve? I didn't have the answers, but I promised myself that I would get them.

My first step was to go to work on a set of company objectives. I turned to the executive committee for help and talked the matter over with my wife. But I quickly discovered what I had suspected from the beginning: Working out objectives was going to be a one-man job—mine.

I started by reviewing company history. This made me realize that I was sometimes too paternalistic. Too often I determined what was best for people on the basis of what I thought they should need and want. I vowed this wouldn't happen in setting objectives. I listened to what the employees, in their many subtle ways, were telling me about their wants and needs.

The company objectives took six months to work out. They proclaimed that Berkley and Company was in business for four basic reasons: (1) to contribute toward a better life for employees and their families; (2) to provide maximum security and a fair return for investors; (3) to be a good citizen in the community, state, and nation; and (4) to provide customers with increasingly better products and better service at competitive prices and always treat them fairly.

The key to achieving these objectives was our ability to carry out the programs that were to back them up. For example, the first objective—to contribute toward a better life for employees—would be supported by 19 programs. They included a health and life insurance program, on-the-job training, and an incentive pay setup for direct production jobs.

Setting objectives and spelling out programs led to decisions on strategy and priorities. These decisions, in turn, focused management's attention on the planning, organization, and control functions. Knowing where we were going and how we were going to get there was a good feeling.

If objectives were good for the company, I reasoned, they ought to be good for me and my family. It's even more important to set personal objectives, I decided. The key question was: What am I, Berkley Bedell, trying to accomplish? It took a year to work out 43 personal objectives. In many ways, they were more difficult to spell out than company objectives. First of all, I had to appraise my life and set a course based on my role, not only as a company president, but also as a father, husband, citizen, and human being. And, second, I ran headlong into the problem of measuring the intangibles that determine personal success.

Three personal objectives were the foundation for all the others: (1) to have a good time and bring fun, happiness, and joy to others; (2) to raise a well-adjusted family, helping them develop so that they will live happy lives and contribute toward making the world a better place in which to live; and (3) to live in such a manner as to cause the world to be a little better because of my having been here.

Did writing out my personal objectives solve all my problems? No. But it did help me put many conflicts over values into a better perspective. I now saw the clear and constant relationship between my company and me, between my role as president and my role as a person. Seeing my objectives down on paper also made me realize how difficult they would be to fulfill. That was January 1963.

By the end of the year we had in operation many of the major programs that were outlined in the company objectives. We had installed a pension and retirement program, an employee stock-purchase plan, a companywide performance appraisal system, and a top management incentive plan based on return on net worth before taxes. We also had established an employee policy and procedure manual, extended job descriptions and standards of performance down to the foreman level, and stepped up our management development efforts.

We told employees at every opportunity how these programs were helping to achieve the company objective calling for a better life for them and their families and how the same programs, in turn, depended on every employee's doing his best to assure continued company profitability. Giving employees the opportunity to purchase stock put this point across more effectively than all the bulletin-board sermons put together.

An employee attitude survey taken late that year produced some personally satisfying replies. Of the 250 employees, 151 filled in and returned the forms—anonymously, of course. To the question, "Are you happy in your job?" 110 replied, "Yes." Only 7 said, "No." I answered every suggestion or complaint through the company newspaper. Odors in the plant and muddy parking lots were the two most frequent complaints. A better ventilating system took care of the first; and the second, although still with us, is getting plenty of attention. Trouble is, we've been expanding the plant so rapidly that every freshly paved parking lot soon gets covered by a piece of building.

All in all, 1963 was one of the company's best years for

sales and profits. My reward came in 1964 when President Johnson presented me with the Small Businessman of the Year award, the first of its kind.

Perhaps the single most important year in our history was 1965. We were growing with a purpose. The company, for years dependent on my personal drive, now began to look more and more like a professionally managed organization. The appointment of four outside specialists, for example, turned our family-style board of directors into a professional board. We appointed a director to head up the reorganized marketing department, added a long-overdue production planning and control department, named a research director to take charge of the expanded research facilities, and installed our first computer and data processing units.

I established standards of performance for my job as president, giving top priority to the planning, profit, and growth objectives. The new emphasis on profitability and growth led to a reappraisal of the traditional corporate strategy that was based on making quality products at lower cost. This was achieved largely through vertical integration in virtually every phase of operation. We draw our own steel wire, produce our own nylon under the Trilene label, and mold our own plastic spools, boxes, and floats. We even print our own catalogs, labels, and display materials.

Some people say that the stress on vertical integration grew out of a corn-country tendency toward self-sufficiency. Perhaps it did. But we feel that doing it ourselves gives us better quality control and greater efficiency.

The new strategy called for the production of top-quality fishing tackle that could be sold at premium prices. We reasoned that fishermen are willing to pay a premium price for fishing gear that gives premium performance. This strategy offered the greatest opportunity to fulfill our profit and growth objectives. It also took advantage of a major breakthrough in fishing-rod design that came out of research.

The new casting rod has the same mathematically perfect curve as a cantilevered beam under load. This eliminates the harmonics problem and produces a smooth, kickback-free cast. We call it the Berkley Para/Metric rod.

In the summer of 1965, we bought Rod'Ac Sport Equipment Company, a California-based rod and reel manufacturer. We added its products to our catalog and made our Para/Metric rod the top of the Rod'Ac line. The acquisition offered great promise but carried its share of problems. Fact is, it temporarily broke our profitable stride. First came the inventory problem. The fishing-line business basically involves wire, spools, and labels. A single fishing rod, however, can have as many as 15 parts—and there are dozens of rods of every type and size. Second came the problems of long-distance management—Gardena, California, to Spirit Lake, Iowa. In 1966, we sold the Rod'Ac building and moved the rod-making operations back home to our new plant in Emmetsburg, Iowa.

Company history probably will describe 1967 as the year we fulfilled three prime objectives: (1) to build our rod-making plant; (2) to improve the efficiency of fishing-rod production; and (3) to put our profits back in line.

We now are the fifth largest tackle manufacturer in the industry, and we plan to keep on growing. From research (we think we spend more on R&D than our competitors combined) will come new products that will help us reach our corporate objective: to double sales and profits every three years.

Did all this happen because I wrote out objectives for me and my company? I think so. We would have survived without them, stumbling into new products as we had done in the past and falling into marketing opportunities by-passed by competitors. Having a purpose, a sense of corporate mission, provided the impetus that spelled the difference between just survival and healthy growth.

As for me, I'm a better manager than I was in 1961 when I sat down with the other presidents at the round table. The company is better managed, growing faster, and heading in a more profitable direction. My job as president is easier and more fun, and employees' attitudes tell us that they approve of what's been happening.

The Urgency of the
Management Development Effort

William M. Allen

Dᴜʀɪɴɢ my years as chief executive of Boeing I have frequently stated my belief that people are our most important, most valuable resource. There is nothing new or profound in this observation, but I feel it's worth repeating.

We estimate that Boeing will need more than 400 top management executives and 2,900 middle and lower-level managers in the next 15 years. To meet these targets, we are pursuing management development programs with a sense of urgency.

Corporate success depends on managers who make the

WɪʟʟɪᴀM M. Aʟʟᴇɴ was President and is now Chairman of the Board, The Boeing Company, Seattle, Washington.

decisions—both major and minor—that determine our present and future course. And the higher their decision-making level, the more important these managers become to the organization.

Developing his company's future managers is clearly one of the chief executive's principal responsibilities. It is up to him to see that the company has a systematic approach to the identification, selection, and development of managers. To help him carry out his responsibility, he must rely on every manager—regardless of level—to be the key factor in motivating and developing his people, and in strengthening their determination for self-development.

I have always believed that the growth of every manager is a continuous process of self-development. I further believe that top management can encourage self-development by offering managers a variety of challenging day-to-day, work-centered experiences, supplemented by more formal training opportunities.

To a considerable extent, managers tend to select themselves for promotion by demonstrating superior performance on the job. For this reason we try to place high-potential people in positions that give them the opportunity to make and support important decisions covering a broad range of activities.

Companywide management development efforts are coordinated through an executive development committee composed of five members of my staff, each of whom heads a major functional area of the company. The committee has two primary responsibilities: first, to identify people with outstanding potential as early in their careers as possible and encourage their rapid self-development; second, to assure us there are always enough qualified managers to provide a choice of candidates for executive positions.

Once a year, division managers report to the committee on the progress of their executive development programs. They evaluate the performance and potential of executives who report directly to them, furnish a list of names of high-potential "comers," discuss the quality and number of candidates available for upper division management positions, review proposed major organizational changes, bring up any important divisional staffing problems, and make suggestions for improving the company's executive development program. Heads of corporate functions also go before the committee to review present and future executive manpower resources in their functional areas throughout the company. These committee reports provide an effective two-way assessment of how well we are meeting total corporate management needs.

We give special attention to identifying outstanding management potential in the 25- to 40-year-old group. Early identification permits us to plan long-term management development programs geared to individual needs and to coordinate them with promotional opportunities throughout the company.

To identify these high-talent people, we seek out men with a record of superior performance in a series of positions of increasing responsibility. We look at men who have achieved substantially above-average salary progression and position advancement and at men who are designated as replacements for executive positions. We also look at men who are being considered for advanced management programs or Sloan Fellowships and at men who have been nominated or chosen by their superiors for incentive awards.

Just recently a group of top-level line and staff managers completed an intensive review of our management development program as a special task-force assignment. The results of their study are currently being implemented. A major innovation is the development of a computerized inventory of management-manpower resources, a company-wide, uniform set of data concerning managers at all levels in the company as well as potential managers.

This inventory will provide for an even greater ability to integrate management development activities into a system enabling the company to forecast requirements, inventory managerial resources, plan future requirements, and track and monitor the development and utilization of our managerial resources. The management development performance of organizations and functions will be measured through inventory outputs and results made available to the executive development committee to enable the members to evaluate the effectiveness of this activity. These data, together with the results of the previously mentioned review sessions, will provide a basis for actions initiated by the committee to assure a continuity of high-caliber managers.

The review sessions have been highly effective in providing information that helps us determine how well executives are performing on their present jobs and whether they have potential for more important responsibilities. They also help us identify those young people who may someday hold key positions in the company's top management. And there's an important byproduct, too. The review sessions help create a corporate environment that stresses our belief in personal growth and development—an important motivator for our managers and a key factor in attracting to Boeing the high-caliber people we seek for the exciting, challenging years ahead.

Marked to Move Up

Bert S. Cross

THERE was a time when the chief executive officer of 3M could walk into the company dining room and identify every executive by name. Those were the days when he could fill a job opening by merely looking around the room for someone ready for promotion. But times have changed, and so has 3M. Today, with 58,000 employees and nearly 60 divisions and subsidiaries worldwide, it is impossible to know personally more than a good handful of executives, anything about their jobs, or the extent to which they are ready for promotion.

As the company grew and daily personal contacts be-

BERT S. CROSS was formerly President, Minnesota Mining and Manufacturing Company, St. Paul, Minnesota. He is now Chairman of the Board and Chief Executive Officer.

tween the chief executive and lower-level executives became a thing of the past, the search for good men ready to
promote turned more and more toward original employment applications, job assignments, pay history, and performance appraisals already in personnel files. The personnel department, quite naturally, became the prime source
of counsel and guidance in selecting executives for promotion. But we soon realized that we were getting to know less
and less about more and more of our executives.

During the 1950's, some of our newer, faster-growing
divisions began looking to other parts of the company for
management talent by asking for names of executives ready
for promotion. About the same time that my predecessor
approached retirement, the board chairman noted that
"when the new chief executive is selected, the problem will
be, not to find *a* man to fill the position, but rather to select
one from the dozen or more capable men in our company."

There were several candidates ready to step into the
chief executive's chair, and the personnel department suggested that a formal, companywide inventory be made, not
only of them, but of executives at all levels ready to move
up. Top management agreed.

We took precautions in setting up the inventory so that
certain things did happen and others did not. Our objective
was to search for and locate potential management talent
for future needs, reaching down below middle management
into the ranks of exempt employees. It was to supply executive manpower where and when needed, but it was not to
create a job-finding operation. We aimed for simplicity.

There was to be no great body of rules and regulations. We were determined that our inventory system would be simple, reasonably low in cost, and strictly confidential.

Three long-held company principles concerning people and promotions underline the mechanics of our inventory:

1. A belief in promoting from within. (Officers have an average of 28 years of 3M service.)
2. A belief that the company can only make management development opportunities available to the executive. In the final analysis, he must develop himself. (The steady growth of the company, of course, opens many opportunities.)
3. A belief in management committees as a source of training. These committees, operating at both corporate and division levels, act as review boards and policy makers for major activities. In this way, executives on operating committees, at first hand, observe and take part in running a large corporation.

Some past practices had to be overcome before we could really make the inventory effective. At first, for example, even our time-honored promotion-from-within policy seemed to be a stumbling block. To many executives, promotion from within meant promotion only from within their departments. It took time and some delicate diplomacy on the part of personnel people to overcome this resistance. But this problem—like others—disappeared as confidence in the inventory grew.

With the basic plan for the inventory agreed on, we made a trial run in a major division. We gathered all the available personal history on a group of salesmen who had been rated as better than average—according to their performance appraisals. The sales manager then added his estimate of each man's management potential. At the same time, he was invited to eliminate any salesman who he thought was not promotable in the near future or to add any new names.

The finished list of better-then-average salesmen included less than 20 percent of the personnel in the unit. Furthermore, many of the salesmen on the list were designated as requiring more experience before being considered promotable. When limited to salesmen promotable within 24 months, the number of men on the list dropped to 5 percent of the total personnel in the unit.

By projecting the growth of the unit and estimating the number of managers needed within two years, we concluded that there was a lack of management potential in this unit. Then we made the same trial in another division —with opposite results. This division, it turned out, had excess management potential.

These experimental runs clearly pointed out that (1) a young, fast-expanding division will not develop managers as rapidly as needed and (2) an older, more stable division will turn out managers faster than it develops opportunities for them. These conclusions, in turn, showed the obvious major point in selling the company-wide inventory program.

Results of the trials were presented to top management, which approved the establishment of the inventory in all divisions. Well-established divisions saw opportunities opening up for their excess management talent in newer, more dynamic divisions. Newer divisions, in turn, saw the inventory as a source of tried and proven executive talent. And another major benefit was the stimulating effect of cross-pollinating divisions with managers from other company areas. This is particularly important for a widely diversified, multiproduct company such as 3M.

Every area of the company contributed names to the inventory and was urged to use the inventory to find the best candidates for openings in its operations. At the same time, we were careful not to dilute the manager's prerogative of choosing his own staff.

There are three types of documents for each manager in the inventory; first, a running history of his performance (a new performance appraisal is filed every year); second, a personal history that describes what the man brought to the company as a new employee, his education and previous employment, and a list of his assignments in the company; and, third, an estimate of potential—what his manager thinks of his future, reviewed and updated at least every two years.

The key document is the estimate of potential. It is a rounded picture of the man's strengths, his interests, and any limitations on promotion, such as health problems or unwillingness to relocate. The manager also recommends the types of jobs or the specific jobs for which he thinks the man is especially qualified. This recommendation is looked at closely but with some reservations, because the manager himself may be limited in his objective knowledge of the requirements for success in the job he is suggesting for his man. Full information is then coded and put on tab cards, and a print-out is made.

A list of candidates for an opening is compiled from a visual search of this print-out. The file on each man is then checked to screen out those who look right from their codings but who, for some reason, are not realistically qualified for the opening. To this list are added the names of any candidates who are considered suited for the opening even though they may not be included in the inventory or, if they are, may not be coded exactly like the others. If the number of candidates selected at this point is too large—say, 50 to 100—the manager looking for the new man may be asked to tighten up his criteria to eliminate weaker candidates. Conversely, if the criteria are so stringent that they produce only one or two candidates, the manager is urged to loosen his standards to produce a longer list of qualified candidates. Ideally, we strive for at least 6 but not more than 20 candidates for each opening.

The inventory gives us a quantitative picture of the promotable group with respect to age, education, and current job and pay levels. There is also a qualitative analysis, along with a breakdown of how the group has changed in mix, the number of interdivision moves triggered by the inventory, the promotion rate for a given part of the executive population, and information on the ratio of resignations to deaths or to retirements.

A picture of executive supply and demand also emerges. The supply is the sum of potential manpower in the inventory. Some parts of this supply are ready now for new responsibilities. These men are called "probables." Others are ready to move on only after more experience on the present job or only into certain types of jobs. These men are called "possibles." Still others are listed as best suited to their present responsibilities. This group, while not likely to move into new responsibilities now, nevertheless forms an important part of our total management talent. We want to know who all are in it and where they are located, for some of them will catch fire again in the future.

The demand side of the picture is determined by projecting future needs for managerial talent. The projection is based largely on division estimates of specific management manpower needs for the coming two years.

A typical search for job candidates works this way. A manager who is looking for a man to fill a job opening sits down with the division salary administrator, outlines the job specifications, and describes the candidate he is looking for. A skillful administrator will get the manager to consider several important points regarding the job specifications: Is the job changing? If so, should the specifications be revised and a new type of candidate sought rather than a duplicate replacement?

With these points settled, the salary administrator goes

to the companywide inventory and gets the list of candidates. At this stage, the candidates' present supervisors must O.K. the release of the files. This is often a delicate, time-consuming operation. A candidate's supervisor may not think the new position is, in fact, a promotion or even an opportunity for his subordinate. He may feel that the candidate has a better job where he is, or that the candidate may be a key man for an opening coming up in the near future in his present department.

With each candidate cleared for promotion, the files are turned over to the searching manager with the admonition that under no circumstances should the candidates be contacted. Ideally, the manager will be happy with the candidates and will narrow his choice to three, with a request for additional information on them. This information usually comes from the candidates' present supervisors, who alone may grant permission for their men to be interviewed. The searching manager then interviews the candidates and makes his choice.

But it doesn't end there. The searching manager may be asked by the other two candidates why they were not chosen. In this way, each rejected candidate discovers his weak points. If he is the right sort of person, he will work out a program with his supervisor to strengthen his background and prepare himself for the next opportunity. But in every case the initiative belongs to the individual. Help is there if he wants it. If he doesn't, then he's not the man we want to promote. And we usually find out soon enough.

As for top management's role in the inventory, our

corporate management committee approves all key appointments at the division level. We insist on seeing at least three candidates for each job opening, two of them preferably from outside the division. Although we usually go along with the recommended first choice, we have at times rejected all three candidates and requested a new set of names. At the very least, we ask a lot of questions to make sure that the three candidates have been carefully picked.

In some ways, our most important role is to make sure that new management blood is being fed into the inventory. While visiting divisions, we look around for new management talent. When we return, we call in the personnel people and tell them about several executives who have impressed us. Are they in the inventory? If not, why not? You can be sure that personnel will go back to the division and ask the same question, adding this suggestion of its own: "Perhaps you should take a closer look at these men."

News that top management is looking for good people and keeping track of them spreads rapidly. This is an important byproduct of the inventory. Throughout the company, managers who deserve to be considered for promotion know they are being considered. This is in line with our original idea of keeping the company's management inventory system as personal as possible. So, in many ways, is our recent decision to take the corporate top management committee to divisions instead of having the division head and his staff travel to corporate headquarters for meetings. It means extra time on the road for me and my staff, but it is worth it. After all, if you are going to measure the value of a manager the best place to do it is in his own backyard.

At present, there are 3,000 names in the inventory, roughly one-quarter of our 12,000 management employees worldwide. This seems to be a workable ratio.

As the company expands (we say the sun never sets on 3M), I often ask myself how we would keep track of our good people in St. Paul or Germany or Japan without the inventory. Particularly encouraging to me is the enthusiasm for the inventory expressed by top management in some of the companies we have established in other countries.

We first entered directly into international markets in 1951, with hardly more than a handful of overseas employees. We now employ about 22,000 nationals at our manufacturing and sales facilities in 34 different countries. As a matter of fact, we have more overseas employees today than there were total employees in 3M just ten years ago. International operations in 1968 accounted for more sales than all of 3M had in 1958.

This kind of growth is stimulated by people who are on their way up. The companywide personnel inventory provides them with an avenue for career growth. That avenue was designed not only to give the overseas employee promotional opportunities within his own company, but also to give him opportunities for transnational promotion to positions in other 3M overseas subsidiaries or the parent company in the United States.

For example, a national who was general sales manager of 3M France is now managing director of our Ferrania operations in Italy. A personnel manager at 3M United Kingdom in Great Britain is now area personnel manager for Europe, stationed at our headquarters in St. Paul. The managing director of our Far Eastern merchandising subsidiaries moved to Hong Kong from Australia, where he had been a sales and marketing director. And a 3M France division manager came to the United States as a division international marketing director and has now moved on to a position of responsibility in our Argentine subsidiary.

The other side of the coin is that domestic management personnel have global opportunities which considerably extend the horizons of their business careers.

It is evident that the personnel inventory enables us to tap a vast reservoir of domestic and international management talent. A secondary benefit of great importance to 3M is the international integration that a multinational company must achieve. This integration can be achieved, in my opinion, only through interchange of personnel.

It's a two-way street, worldwide, with winners going in both directions. Our people like it, and so do I. I don't think 3M could get along without the inventory. We don't intend to try.

Should You Have
an Executive Vice President?

William H. McElwain

Should there be an executive vice president in the average company? As a former executive vice president, I don't think so.

The position of executive vice president belongs in a one-on-one type of organization in which each departmental head has an understudy who is obviously being trained to take his job. When the right men are picked for the "second jobs," the organization takes on depth and the men receive valuable on-the-job training that pays off *if* the

William H. McElwain is President, Jersey Central Power & Light Company and New Jersey Power & Light Company, Morristown, New Jersey.

second men get their promotions. It is precisely because of this "if" that I question the value of an executive vice president.

Let us first look at a company that does not have an executive vice president, but in which the heir apparent to the presidency emerges naturally and logically. In a company with a conventional organizational setup, each vice president is directly responsible to the president. If the company has a compulsory retirement policy, speculation as to which VP gets the "brass ring" when the president retires can be pretty interesting.

There is always the possibility, of course, that someone may be brought in from outside. But what normally happens is this: If there is a real leader among the vice presidents, he is recognized as such not only at his own level but throughout the organization.

As time passes, his peers look to him for help with their own problems, and more and more problems unrelated to his own sphere of responsibility flow normally to him. He seems automatically to become the group's choice as their leader. Because his associates seek him out to discuss their problems, their cooperation—if he becomes president—is practically assured.

The transition, therefore, of one of the group's peers from a position at their own level to that of their superior is accomplished with relatively few problems. Although the procedure may not be consistent, this is the way it happens in many organizations.

Now let's look at the other side of the coin. Assuming,

for the sake of discussion, that the position is a beneficial one both to the individual and to the company, what do we see going on in an organization that does have the position of executive vice president?

There are some advantages—on the surface, at least. With such a title in the corporate setup, the image of the company, both to shareholders and to members of the organization, is one of management depth. It says that the board of directors has come to grips with the problem of providing the company with future top management. It says there is now an authoritative post for decision making in case of the chief executive's absence or illness. And it assures shareholders that there will be continuity of management policy in the event of changes in top management. The transition, it says, will take place smoothly, with no major disruptions.

But what about the man who holds the title? There is no question that the man appointed to the position of executive vice president receives valuable on-the-job training that is particularly important to himself and the organization—if he eventually takes the next step up. While this on-the-job training certainly has its value, whether or not it is necessary is another question.

Once an individual becomes executive VP, there are two distinct approaches he can take. First, he can pursue the course of not delving into the responsibilities of his former associates on his own initiative. Instead, he will wait for them to come to him for advice and assistance. If he is the right kind of person for the job, the vice presidents will have come to him before his promotion, and they will continue to come to him afterward. Thus he will naturally continue to stay close to the overall affairs of the company. That is one approach.

The executive vice president can, on the other hand, be a "take charge" kind of person. By applying his personal drive and using the authority that goes with his title, he can succeed in having all the corporate affairs go through his hands, thereby pretty much insulating the president from day-to-day problems. If the executive vice president takes this approach, the line between success and failure can be a very fine one.

He can alienate his former associates by keeping too tight a rein on their functions. At the same time, he can give the president the idea that he is a young whippersnapper just waiting to get into his chair. So, as a result of troubles from both his subordinates and his superior, the take-charge executive VP can be an also-ran when the new president is chosen.

Despite these complications, do you still think you should have an executive vice president in your organization? My own feeling is that the position is a needless and dangerous one.

If there is a real leader among the vice presidents, they continually bring him their problems; so his knowledge of company affairs is already broad. Hence the value of training he receives as executive vice president is questionable.

There is no doubt in my mind that the position of executive vice president is a difficult one to work from. It is very easy to alienate not only your own associates but the top man himself. And, if that happens, both the organization and the individual are losers.

I didn't like the tightrope I had to walk when I was executive vice president. What about you? Would you settle for the position of senior vice president in your company?

Getting the Most
Out of the Board

George S. Dively

IT SEEMS to me that a great deal can be done to increase the effectiveness of the board of directors. Yet the chief executive who tries to make his company's board more effective probably will not find much help in traditional management sources.

For some reason, many of the advances in professional management over the past several decades appear to have bypassed the board room. There is no large body of knowledge on the subject, few well-documented case histories,

GEORGE S. DIVELY is Chairman of the Board, Harris Intertype Corporation, Cleveland, Ohio. He was President of the company from 1947 to 1961.

few consultants who claim special experience or ability in this area. Perhaps more of us should be sharing what we have learned through years of experience.

A chairman or president new to his post quickly discovers that working with the board is a job he will have to learn to handle pretty much by himself. If he does adequate research in selecting the directors, if he runs an effective board, and if the company prospers, he then can feel with some justification that he knows something about the board. But perhaps only *his* board. He will find out soon enough that there are many different kinds of boards and different ways of running them. Even his own company, as it evolves or grows, may require a drastically different kind of board at various stages.

I learned this simple but elusive truth from my own experience. Back in the forties, Harris-Intertype was a small, family-controlled company with one basic product— offset printing presses. We had a heavily inside board. Then the decision to diversify and grow was made and management was reorganized. Harris-Intertype now is a publicly owned, professionally managed, medium-sized company with diversified but related product lines in the communications equipment field, both printed and electronic. Today we have a twelve-man board: eight outside and four inside directors. This balance seems about right— for now. In a different company, or at another stage of development in our own company, a different mix might be desirable.

In any event, I believe that neither a wholly inside nor a

wholly outside board (except, of course, for the chief executive) is sound in the long run. An inside board is likely to lack objectivity and perspective. An outside board has difficulty in fully evaluating what is really going on in the company and, as a result, may have trouble when it comes to such vital matters as deciding on top management succession.

But, no matter what the mix, the choice of director must be a good one. Reversing a poor decision is usually difficult and embarrassing. Place particular emphasis on the candidate's experience, his corporate specialty, his interest in your company, and on the type of company he represents. Don't gamble on unknowns. A good director is a special breed of man. He is a respected leader. He has integrity and character, and he has proven ability.

Chief executives generally make good directors. They understand what responsibility at the top means. We try to have at least two outside directors who are chief executives of companies in comparable—but not in the same—fields. As you might expect, they are the most difficult to recruit. They are busy with their own companies, and they are much in demand for all kinds of outside activities.

The best approach to recruiting a chief executive, in my experience, is an appeal to his natural desire to be an even more effective leader in his own company. Compensation for him is usually a secondary consideration. He may be looking for prestige. More likely, he wants to broaden his own background and experience by exposure to other directors and to solutions of other companies' problems. This is probably his single most important reason for joining the board.

Many directors also come from the ranks of lawyers, bankers, and educators. They usually have special relationships with the company that result in an active and continuing interest in its progress. It is sometimes necessary to use discretion to avoid duplicating talent in this area. Our present board includes a top man from each of these professions.

Boards might be more effective if directors could take on special company projects and board committee chairmanships and really work on them. Most directors, unfortunately, are too busy running their own businesses. This is why I feel there is a real need for "professional" corporate directors. The professional director has that unique breadth of outlook that comes from an extensive background which includes many years' experience in successfully running one or more businesses. He also has the special skills and the desire to move from straight-line executive work into a top management advisory capacity. He is willing to serve on a number of boards—perhaps five or more—and to give each sufficient time to permit him to do an effective job.

Chief executives in early retirement, for example, may make ideal professional directors. There are hints of a trend in this direction. I feel this should be encouraged, from both the corporate and individual viewpoints.

A good director can be counted on to ask the right question at the right time, instead of preaching a sermon that usually begins with, "This is how we did it at. . . ."

He is often a sophisticated critic who knows how to support his opinions with reason and facts. A good director does not avoid telling a chief executive what he thinks. And, if he thinks a chief executive is not doing a good job, he should tell him—first in private conversation and then, if necessary, with appropriate follow-through.

Avoid the gripers. The world is full of them. Stay away from the soft-soapers, too. They are more pleasant but just about as harmful. Do encourage lots of frank, wide-open discussion in areas of new policy and others involving special judgment. Outside directors should know your company, your competitors, and your industry. But keep them out of day-to-day operations. They should depend on inside directors and other executives (when coordinated through the chairman) to provide operating details and any internal reports or expertise required.

In my opinion, boards are most effective for evaluating new ideas and proposals and for deciding major questions requiring objective and composite judgment. The directors, of course, must be given all the necessary facts and enough time to think them through. Springing new subjects for action at board meetings usually produces confusion. Put your proposals down on paper and outline the principal alternatives. Adequate facts sometimes dictate decisions.

At Harris-Intertype, we schedule board meetings a year in advance. Each director receives the agenda and all important reports about two weeks beforehand. Some directors come to the board room early to review material in the director's manual, which is prepared for each of them.

The manual includes all previously distributed material, additional information, and any last-minute items.

Board meetings should seldom last more than two hours. If they run longer, this may be a sign that they are poorly planned and the directors inadequately briefed.

I believe the effectiveness of the board can be further increased if directors will periodically evaluate the board's own performance. This can be done in a special one- or two-day meeting held once a year. The directors should discuss how well the board is functioning, what steps can be taken to increase its effectiveness, and what the board can do to improve its contribution to the company's long-term thinking.

Off and on over the past several years, the Harris-Intertype board has been meeting to spell out the responsibilities of directors. We feel that hammering out these responsibilities in written form has produced a better understanding of what directors can and should do to fulfill the board's function most effectively.

Compensation of board members is a sensitive, and somewhat irrational, matter. The usual practice of paying all outside directors on an equal basis might be carefully re-examined in view of their varying specialties, backgrounds, and motivation. Unlike the outside director who is chief executive of a company, a professional corporate director should be fully paid for his services. Proper compensation provides both incentive and prestige. Inside directors should in my opinion not receive extra compensation for serving on the board.

Harris-Intertype's present practice is to pay outside directors a basic annual fee, plus travel expenses. Out-of-town directors receive an additional sum for each board meeting or other company meeting they attend. Additional compensation is paid to directors who are chairmen of board committees and to those who do other special work for the company.

To help maintain a desirable age mix on the board, we have established a written retirement policy: 65 years for inside directors, 70 for outside directors and the chief executive of the company.

We have found that these policies help the board carry out its duties as (1) trustees for the shareholders' investment, (2) the broad policy-making body of the corporation, and (3) selectors of, and advisers to, the chief executive of the company. These duties are outlined in the following statement of responsibilities:

GENERAL LEGAL RESPONSIBILITIES

1. *Broad policy determination and overall operations.* Exercise the general powers as the governing body of the corporation with limits defined by statute, charter, and bylaws. In this connection, directors are responsible for broad policies and general operations of the corporation. While operating duties and decisions are generally delegated to officers, directors must retain their overall responsibilities for corporate performance.

2. *Relationship to shareholders.* Serve as trustees for all of the shareholders. Acts of directors are subject to the same

standards of fidelity, good faith, and subordination of private interests that apply to trustees generally.

3. *Corporate knowledge.* Be sufficiently familiar with the affairs of the corporation to be able to exercise the judgment of a reasonably prudent man.

4. *Officers.* Elect the corporate officers.

5. *Meetings.* Meet at sufficiently frequent intervals to discharge the duties for which directors are held responsible. Directors may take action at a meeting, or in certain cases by instrument in writing without a meeting, but cannot act by proxy.

SPECIFIC DUTIES AND RESPONSIBILITIES

1. *Shareholders.* Represent all the shareholders as trustees for their investment. Advise generally on shareholder relationships.

2. *Policies.* Establish broad corporate policies, usually but not exclusively upon recommendation of the chief executive officer.

3. *Chief executive officer.* Elect the chief executive officer and delegate management responsibility and authority to him. Appraise his effectiveness and establish his compensation. Provide continuity in that office.

4. *Other officers.* Upon recommendation of the chief executive officer, and through or in collaboration with the management development committee, elect other corporate officers, approve their compensation, and generally appraise their performance.

5. *Committees.* Upon recommendation of the chairman, appoint, define the powers of, and dissolve committees of the board.

6. *Dividends.* Establish dividend policy and take dividend actions.

177

7. *Financing.* Approve overall financing programs, subject to authorization by shareholders when necessary. Authorize appropriate officers to take actions as may be required to implement such programs.

8. *Acquisitions and mergers.* Approve acquisitions and mergers, subject to authorization by shareholders when necessary. Suggest acquisition possibilities.

9. *Capital investments.* Review and approve regular capital investment guide programs annually and authorize special individual capital investments exceeding $200,000.

10. *Disposal of capital assets.* Approve any action involving disposal of a capital asset in excess of $50,000.

11. *Contributions.* Authorize contributions above $50,000 each and annually ratify other contributions.

12. *Long-term commitments.* Authorize all leases of more than 10 years' duration, or involving payments of over $50,000 per year, and all pension and retirement plans. Annually review lease liabilities, pension and retirement plans, insurance coverages, and loan guarantees.

13. *Planning.* Critically review and advise on long- and short-range planning of the corporation. Periodically evaluate progress against such plans.

14. *Corporate relations.* Review and make suggestions on building and maintaining constructive financial, trade, employee, and public relations and a favorable corporate image.

15. *Ethical and professional standards.* Assure, through continuing review, that directors, officers, and other employees act in accordance with established and accepted ethical and professional standards.

16. *Knowledge of company and industry.* Keep informed on the company's business and, to the extent feasible, on the industries in which the company operates.

17. *Meetings.* Attend board meetings and meetings of committees to which appointed.

18. *Board membership*. In collaboration with the chairman and management development committee, propose to the shareholders annually the size and make-up of the board and fill interim vacancies.

19. *Auditors*. Recommend outside auditing firm to be voted upon by shareholders.

20. *Bylaws*. Establish and approve changes in bylaws, subject to shareholder authorization as required.

SPECIAL CONTRIBUTIONS EXPECTED OF OUTSIDE DIRECTORS

1. *Experience*. Bring to the board objectivity and breadth of specialized and other relevant experience.

2. *Consultation*. Serve as consultants to chief executive officer and, with his approval, to others in the company.

3. *Advice and criticism*. Offer constructive advice and criticism and promote actions which are in the best interests of the corporation.

4. *New business*. Be on the lookout for new business generally and assist in specific customer contacts when requested to do so.

5. *Independent forum*. As an informal group, provide an independent forum to which management should demonstrate continuous accountability for overall policies and actions.

SPECIAL CONTRIBUTIONS EXPECTED OF INSIDE DIRECTORS

1. *Objectivity*. Assist the chief executive officer in providing balance and objectivity in the board and in the corporation. In this connection, inside directors should serve interests of entire company rather than their own area of responsibility.

2. *Reflect board to company.* Reflect the general thinking of the board to the company.

3. *Information to outside directors.* With the concurrence of the chief executive officer, provide outside directors with relevant information about company operations as required.

4. *Top management exposure.* Provide exposure of top management to other directors for continuing evaluation.

CAUTIONS FOR DIRECTORS

1. *Interference.* Having delegated responsibility and authority to corporate officers, avoid interference with actual operations.

2. *Internal politics.* Avoid "rump sessions" and "internal politics" between members of the board—particularly applicable to combinations of inside and outside directors.

3. *Confidential information.* Avoid disclosing confidential information about the company to unauthorized persons.

4. *Continuation of service.* Periodically initiate individual discussions with the chairman concerning own contributions as a board member.

A Long, Hard Look
at Your Management

S. Clark Beise

S<small>EATED</small> around a conference table, several bank officers were examining audit reports and other statistical data on a corporation that was applying for a loan.

"These reports look fine," said one of the bank officers. "But what about the future? What are the corporate objectives? What is management doing to achieve them? And what about management itself? How good is it?"

Scenes such as this are being repeated with growing frequency at meetings of lending officers in banks across

S. C<small>LARK</small> B<small>EISE</small> is Chairman, Executive Committee, Bank of America National Trust and Savings Association, San Francisco. He was formerly President of the company.

the country. For, during recent years, corporate management has been coming in for steadily increasing appraisal in the loan-making process. Financial statements continue to be of vital importance to lending institutions. But, as a banker, I can state unequivocally that a bank's appraisal of company management is a crucial factor in the decision to grant or deny a loan application.

The three C's—character, capacity, and capital—are still as fundamental to credit evaluation as are the three R's to our basic educational process. Assuming that we all recognize the importance of character and capital, let us explore that word sandwiched in the middle—capacity—the organized potential of a company to grow and prosper. Let's call it *management*.

The analysis of management as part and parcel of credit analysis is increasing for a number of reasons. Commercial banks are placing even greater emphasis on this kind of analysis as competition from domestic and international markets grows more intense; as taxation problems increase and become more complex; as government exercises more control over our world economy; and as profits are challenged by increased costs from many directions.

World War II was the springboard that made us management-conscious. In the prewar days, the management image of many companies tended to blend with the men or families that ran them. As the technology and mass-production techniques born of the war were further spurred by expanding international markets and the resulting business upheaval, the management picture also changed. Company founders and owners died or retired, and many old-time presidents who reputedly could keep track of every corporate detail were replaced by the "management team." This process was accelerated as the pace of public ownership of corporate stock increased and became a requirement for growth.

I don't want to imply that a personal or family management is necessarily obsolete or undesirable. There are many examples of outstanding performances in these categories. But there are also cases where companies have looked primarily to small circles of friends and relatives, often neglecting to consider seriously the need for capable, continuous management. Too often, these companies have not been able to keep pace with the volatile conditions of today's shrinking world.

True, management teams may leave much to be desired. There are some recent dramatic examples of deterioration of management in "good name" companies with good records. These companies have been unable to cope with changes that are taking place. Moreover, there are companies with strong financial positions whose managements are "standing on the record." That usually means they are stodgy and living in the past. On the other side, we can find companies that rely too much on youthful energy. And we can also find many companies with mediocre financial positions that have good futures because of excellent management. Thus management assumes special importance and takes on unusual complexity when we consider extending credit.

Because of the size of our bank, we are able to make loans in all areas of the economy. Yet we have found that businesses of widely diverse natures possess similar management characteristics that we can explore, compare, and evaluate. Our management analysis concentrates on uncovering the skills, talents, and strengths (and sometimes weaknesses) in seven corporate areas:

1. *Flexibility*. This is perhaps the most important management element. Does management possess— or has it indicated—the capacity to adjust alertly, intelligently, and effectively to changing conditions? Today we need people to prevent problems, not just people who are simply solving problems. Management problem-solving techniques are becoming more and more limited, and problem prevention is becoming a major objective.

2. *Management depth*. Management today isn't just the president or a couple of top officers. There should be an organized team. This team may now be extremely capable, but are there replacements in reserve for front-line action? Are there age problems and experience gaps in line for the future? We hear that there is no pure white or black—only different shades of gray. Some forward-looking managements have gone beyond the blacks, whites, and grays to analyze their management depth graphically. By using a scale of colors matched to degrees

of performance, an organizational diagram can be keyed to show how management is performing in each specific area of responsibility. A diagram with a preponderance of color denoting excellence in present performance and ample ready reserves is a pleasure to see, both for the president of the company and for his banker.

3. *Planning.* What are management's long-term and short-term goals? How are these objectives being achieved? Some companies, because they lack well-defined objectives, merely spin their wheels. Others, with established objectives valid under one set of economic conditions, often fail to realize that these conditions may change markedly.

Again, do the people in management understand the company's objectives? Are their programs and projects properly oriented? A person who doesn't know what he's supposed to do can never know whether or not he is successful. You can have a payroll and an organization chart, but with no objective you have no real organization. Are the principal functions of the organization effectively coordinated, or is one function, such as marketing or production, disproportionately important to the detriment of the organization as a whole?

4. *Research and development.* Does management recognize that today's research pennies may be tomorrow's sales dollars? Is the company oriented toward

research and development? Is it getting its money's worth, or is it merely sending research funds down the drain?

5. *Organizational structure.* Does the structure lend itself to quick, dynamic action, or is it overinsulated by excessive levels of supervision? Do line and staff conflict to the detriment of lower supervisory levels? Is the span of supervision excessive, leading to management inertia? Is excessive centralized authority inhibiting efficiency of line operations?

6. *Standards.* Is there organizational discipline? Are there high internal and external standards of performance? Is actual performance measured against standards of excellence, and is remedial action taken when it is indicated? Are projections of sales and experience properly utilized and objectively compared periodically as to results?

7. *Personnel policies.* Are there personnel policies for hiring and training management personnel and upgrading personnel to senior management positions? Are seniority problems serious? Is there a shortage of new blood and new ideas? Is compensation adequate for what is expected? How is morale?

These seven areas overlap in many ways, but two important essentials in our economic world today are superimposed over all of them: continuous appraisal of management performance and forward planning for future decisions.

A transcontinental airline pilot plans his objective and course in advance. But without checking his position and adjusting en route he is not likely to arrive as planned—if at all! It is also essential that we set goals. But all goal and no achievement is sometimes the situation.

Management today is a marketable commodity, and it can serve as important security for a loan. The value depends on how well management plans and performs. All management decisions are financial. Sooner or later, they all end up in the company books as profit or loss. But by that time it's often too late.

The corporate president, as a matter of enlightened self-interest, might well turn the mirror on his own company and appraise its management as his banker might. The results might astound him.

How to Get into the
Financial Blue Book

Lewis B. Cullman

Lᴉᴋᴇ high society, the financial community has its own select circle—those companies whose stock is "approved for purchase" by large institutions. In presenting his case for recognition and its rewards, a president can expect no mercy from the financial world. His company's record and his own performance as chief executive will be severely judged.

Speaking as a member of the financial community, I feel that too many presidents give too little thought to how they present their company story. They don't fully realize

Lᴇᴡɪs B. Cᴜʟʟᴍᴀɴ is President, Lewis B. Cullman, Inc., investment advisors, New York City.

188

that a favorable impression can have important dollars-and-cents advantages in terms of lower interest rates and a higher price-earnings ratio for the company's stock, thus creating greater opportunities for acquisitions and mergers.

Too many chief executives think of the financial community as a necessary evil to be kept at arm's length unless and until needed. Even after a decade of growing public interest in the stock market, many presidents still characterize their feelings in this way: "I'm in business to sell my product, not to sell stock." Or, "I want to raise profits, not the price of the stock." They are right to the extent that stock prices should not be a prime concern, but stock prices are a fact of life and cannot be summarily dismissed.

Although most company presidents aren't this short-sighted, many who seek strong support in the financial community don't give the gaining of it nearly enough thought and planning. They never really learn the rules of the game or develop a long-range program to provide mutual funds, brokerage houses, insurance companies, and banks with sufficient information to determine the profits and potential growth of their companies. But, after neglecting this job, these same presidents—when they need financial support—are usually the ones most likely to complain that "Wall Street doesn't understand our problems."

What should a chief executive do to get his story across? I wish I could offer a handy rule of thumb that fits companies of every size and situation. I cannot. There are, however, several approaches that should be considered.

Perhaps the most neglected point, though a seemingly obvious one, is to know what information a financial community representative wants. Too often, managers who would never think of selling a new $1.98 product without extensive market research will attempt to explain their company to a man considering a $10-million investment without working out a realistic and logical presentation. Even worse, they may try to satisfy a sophisticated securities analyst with incomplete answers and overoptimistic guesses of a kind they would never allow to be made to a customer's purchasing agent.

One of the worst errors is a tendency to overestimate sales and earnings. A number of companies listed on the New York Stock Exchange have done great damage to their reputations in the financial community in this way. As a result, almost everything they now say is suspect. Of course, I don't mean to imply that a company's earnings can always match its chief executive's predictions, but a pattern of wide error destroys confidence.

To financial men, the ability to make successful projections of future earnings and profits is an important measure of top management. It shows that the president has a real grasp of industry conditions and that the company can meet economic shifts and overcome unexpected situations. Besides accuracy in predicting a company's growth rate, a fairly steady pattern is likely to make a favorable impression. I think that the best companies grow at an even pace. There are exceptions when a firm such as Xerox makes a sudden technological breakthrough. But, generally speaking, sudden increases make me wary because they can often lead to unexpected adjustments in earnings later on.

Despite the most conservative projections, a chief executive may well turn out to be wide of the mark. The best answer here is to admit the fact and try to be more accurate in the future. Too many executives try to sugarcoat unfavorable developments. They blame the weather, a raw material supplier's strike, unexpected R&D costs, or any one of an infinite number of unforeseen circumstances for their companies' poor performance. Financial institutions know these problems exist and are suspicious of a chief executive who offers them as excuses too often. After all, anticipating and adjusting to problems is one of his main jobs.

Here are a few other factors that have a negative effect on me: I'm always a little wary of companies that have complicated leasing arrangements for their equipment or very involved capitalization plans. In my experience, many of these financial techniques are of value only to the people who recommend them, not to the company using them. I also regard it as a lack of common sense when a company has excessive amounts of idle cash in its bank account. An astute management usually finds ways to keep this cash working—for example, by buying short-term securities. I get a hint of a lack of financial wisdom when companies seem unwilling to consider borrowing money for expansion or other worthwhile reasons. A company that dilutes its stock needlessly to avoid debt is bound to lose the interest of financial institutions that may be interested in its stock.

But most damning of all in the financial community is

a chief executive who can't or won't recognize and explain his business's prospects and problems. Here is an example of what I mean: I once visited a clothing manufacturer who specialized in cotton knit goods. He had a very persuasive and well-documented story to show that his part of the garment industry was not really affected by style changes. Some of his arguments sounded pretty good. Ignoring a surprisingly poor year, however, he kept insisting that his ideas were still sound. The fact was, a basic style change had finally overtaken his part of the industry, and he could never hope to maintain his business unless he took drastic action.

Some companies have a good story to tell and don't even realize it. Instead, they stick to an outdated description of their business. The president of a manufacturing company, for example, explained again and again that he was selling to a budget-priced market. At the time, however, this market was entering a period of intense competition and sharply decreased profits. What the president neglected to mention was that he had already committed his company quite successfully to new high-profit specialty and distribution areas. To the security analyst, this would have made an investment story of much greater appeal.

While every company must put its best foot forward for the financial world, the ideal situation is one in which the company is firmly established in some protected area of an industry. This may be by virtue of patents, a unique distribution system, or a special combination of factors. Finding this kind of protected range to graze on is particularly important for the smaller company that hopes for recognition in the financial community.

Sometimes a unique product can be enough to attract wide financial support and investor interest while the company is still relatively small. Xerox and Polaroid are obvious examples. Avon, on the other hand, confounded the skeptics in the dog-eat-dog cosmetics industry by proving that cosmetics could be sold door to door.

In a few cases, a company can be appealing primarily on the basis of its management methods. Though Bobbie Brooks, Inc. is in the garment industry—one that has never enjoyed much favor with the financial community—it was able to achieve a special status. Its president proved that he could use advanced management techniques in accounting, production controls, and long-range planning so that predictions of growth could be made accurately and met consistently.

The companies that will have the greatest opportunities to apply these lessons in the near future will be service industries. A few advertising agencies, for example, have already gone public and won financial support even though they are in what traditionally has been thought of as a highly volatile industry. A dramatic example of what a service industry can do is supplied by a pest-control firm in Georgia. Although its sales and earnings had risen steadily for years, it failed to attract interest and support on Wall Street. Suddenly, its market value was discovered when the president put over the idea that the company was a nonregulated utility and should have a price-earnings ratio in line with other utilities, even though it provided exterminating service instead of power or water.

Once a president realizes *how* to put his company's story across, the tough job of *getting* it across still remains. It is not enough to wait for people to come knocking at your door. Nor does it make sense to sit tight until you want to go public, arrange a merger, set up a large line of credit, or place a big block of stock with an institutional investor. A five-year record of steady growth is usually enough to get an interested hearing, but much of the value of this kind of record is lost if it is trotted out at the end of the period with the boast, "Look how well we've done." It takes time to build a reputation in the financial community, no matter how well you've done.

The ways of communicating with financial institutions are by no means clear-cut, although there are a few basic things that can be done by companies big or small, privately or publicly held. A good beginning for companies that have had little contact with the financial community is an active search for opportunities to be evaluated and recognized. One way is to establish relationships with banks and other lending institutions to improve your credit reputation. Another way is to widen the distribution of senior securities by calling them to the attention of insurance companies, pension funds, and other investors. It is always good policy for smaller companies to concentrate initially on institutions located near them before moving on to those in distant financial centers.

Smaller publicly held companies can follow the same general advice in seeking wider stock distribution. Until recently, many of these companies have been put off by the idea that the key to wider distribution of stock seemed to be the New York market. With the growth of mutual funds and the proliferation of institutional investors all over the country, there is now a great opportunity for an undervalued company to widen its stock distribution. Brokerage houses in Cleveland, Washington, D.C., and other cities now maintain indices of the prices of local company issues. Getting listed in these groups is a good way to attract the attention of investors. Financial institutions are coming to realize that since most of the glamour companies of the 1950's were located in the East and West, these waters are pretty well fished out. They are now looking for good companies in the Middle West and South.

For a president with a really outstanding story to tell about his company, generous investments of time and energy in attracting the interest of the financial community will turn ultimately to one objective—getting its stock on the "approved for purchase" list of major financial institutions. When a company attracts the attention of these institutions, passes the critical evaluation of their securities analysts, and is selected for acquisition, it has won its spurs in the financial community.

More important to the average company is the fact that once it makes the "approved for purchase" list of one or more insurance companies or mutual funds, it is likely to be added to the lists of other banks, brokerage houses, and financial advisers for recommendation to their customers. In addition to improving the price and price-earnings ratio of the company's stock, the approval of the financial community tends to have an effect in the marketplace, helping to sell the favored firm's products and services.

While there has been a close historical relationship between large blue-chip companies and institutional investors, there is no longer any real prejudice in this respect. Major institutional recognition is available to many smaller and medium-sized companies if they can get their message across and meet certain standards. Here are two of the more common criteria: (1) An annual net income of at least $1 million. Given a return on sales of 5 percent, this translates to a volume of at least $20 million. (2) At least $10 million of market value. If net profit is $1 million and the price-earnings ratio is 20, at least half the stock must be in the hands of the investing public, not locked up in family or management accounts.

While these financial criteria are often the bare minimum needed to attract the interest of major financial institutions, a chief executive must not forget that figures alone will never be enough. The assessment of his company will be based on an analysis of cold statistics and an evaluation of warm bodies. And, in most cases, the president is the only one who can really put over the effective story of his company's past performance and future prospects.

The job of "selling" a company to the financial community is a demanding and often protracted pursuit that no chief executive can afford to neglect. Because the business benefits are great, the top management of a company that has not received its full measure of recognition cannot truly be said to be operating at full capacity.

Is There a Secret to Growth?

Robert O. Barber

For the jaded businessman in his forties who wants to raise the excitement level of his job, I recommend the following: With three of your associates scrape together all your assets and purchase working control in your company from the founding family. Then, two months later, find yourself in a price war that removes 35 percent of company revenues and reduces the value of your investment by more than half.

All this happened in 1955 to me and three other members of the top management of Univis, Inc. (then Univis Lens Company). Sales that year were slightly over $4 mil-

Robert O. Barber is president of Univis, Inc., Fort Lauderdale, Florida.

lion. Our operating loss was $290,000. We had $1.3 million in assets and $1.7 in debts. The market value of company shares outstanding was slightly over $1 million. That was the nature of our crisis.

Much of the company's progress since those troubled days ten years ago, we feel, is the happy result of corporate planning. We started by taking an objective look at the company's strengths and weaknesses and its image in the marketplace. A management engineering firm helped us research our markets and plan for product diversification. An opinion research organization took on the job of finding out what our customers and others really thought of us. We analyzed and appraised our assets in terms of technological know-how, management skills, and company reputation, as well as in terms of tangibles that show up on the balance sheet.

Among our many strengths was a reputation for quality products and constructive policies. There were a few weak areas, too. For one thing, former policy-level management had failed to look ahead. Patents had expired, but nobody seemed to worry because "no one knows how to make eyeglass lenses as well as Univis does." In addition, a substantial portion of our sales was made to the distribution outlets of our two largest competitors, who, as a result, had the power to plunge us into a loss position by simply stopping their purchases.

Information from these studies helped us chart our future course, but our immediate concern was to put Univis in the black. As a start, we established a cost-cutting program that eliminated most of the fat while sparing most of the muscle. We wrote job descriptions for all jobs and set up performance standards for key people. For the past several years these standards have been the basis for the payment of incentive bonuses.

We spelled out our company creed—the first in our history—and defined our business: "Univis, Inc. is engaged in providing products and services used in the protection and improvement of human vision." This statement changed management's concepts and broadened the horizon for future planning and growth.

We established corporate objectives for three years ahead and then broke them down into division objectives. For the same three years, we forecast profit-and-loss statements, balance sheets, and cash flow and revamped our organization chart to show the jobs that would be required to run the company. We established an executive inventory, incorporating training programs to provide the management manpower and skill levels that our expansion programs would require.

Because we believed that decisions are never any better than the information on which they are based, we set up controls to give managers at all levels timely and adequate, but not excessive, information about the jobs for which they were responsible. We formed a management committee composed of top management and division heads to review company performance each month and to report on division achievements as well as problems. The committee has become an excellent management training ground and has formed the base for building a professional management team. Besides their regular committee responsibilities, committee members also study, discuss, and practice problem-solving and decision-making techniques. Each member is a company stockholder and represents a level of competence that provides back-up for top management jobs in the years ahead.

In 1956, we made a small profit—an encouraging sign in view of our problems. Our hopes for turning the company around brightened. Our results in 1957 made our hopes brighter still. And, as 1958 and 1959 brought new record sales and earnings, it was obvious that the recovery program was paying off. The big question before management now changed from "Can we continue to exist?" to "How fast can we grow?"

As the company continued to grow stronger, we discovered that selling eyeglass lenses but no eyeglass frames is like selling gasoline at a service station but no oil. So we purchased three small frame companies, the latest in 1962, and entered the frame business. Our frame volume today alone is larger than the company's entire revenue in 1955.

Toward the end of the 1950's, we realized that the company was outgrowing its Dayton, Ohio, headquarters. A facilities survey showed we would need a new plant to meet future product requirements as well as demands for more room for head-office staff.

We surveyed 14 plant sites in the East and picked Fort Lauderdale, Florida. It put us nearer to our principal lens plant in Puerto Rico, which we set up in 1951 and built into the world's largest producer of improved-type multifocal lenses. We occupied the new plant late in 1960. The move cut into revenues and earnings slumped in 1960—the only year under present management when earnings did not increase. The move paid off, however, and earnings increases were resumed in 1961.

In 1962 we organized an electronics company. This was our first step out of our traditional business into what we considered a promising and related field—electro-optics.

At the end of 1962, the executive committee reviewed the company's progress. On the committee were the executive vice president and treasurer; the first vice president, who controlled all research and engineering activities; and I. We were the three surviving members of the party of four who had started living dangerously back in 1955.

The record showed that company revenues had increased from $4.2 million in 1955 to more than $10.3 million in 1962. From a one-cent-per-share loss in 1955 we had reached the point where we earned $1.01 per share in 1962, adjusted to cover a three-for-two stock split and two stock dividends.

We had also formed a subsidiary company for the manufacture of plastic lenses and other plastic products. This company, Applied Plastics Corporation, was growing and showed indications of being able to diversify into fields that could make it larger and more profitable than its parent.

Univis had produced and marketed the first plastic eyeglass lenses in the late 1940's. But materials then available, while shatterproof and only half the weight of their glass counterparts, nevertheless scratched too easily. We withdrew plastic lenses from the market until more abrasive-resistant materials became available. We reintroduced them in 1960, and in 1964 we introduced improved-type multifocal lenses in plastic. Both products have won ready acceptance. It was obvious that these products formed a new and important field calling for more planning.

Clearly, the company's progress since 1955 was primarily the result of planning. However, much of our planning was intuitive. Forecasts were not sufficiently sophisticated, and our objectives were not formalized in the way they should have been. We realized that the employment of capital in the years ahead would assume a new and greater significance, and we needed constraints which would help guide future decisions.

Our planning covered three years. We knew it had to be extended to at least five years. The job of planning had grown beyond the available time and specialized knowledge of management. We decided to set up a department of formal corporate planning and to bring in a corporate planner to head it up. In September 1963, therefore, we appointed a director of corporate planning (he is now an assistant vice president).

The planning director's first assignment was to study the company's organization and its decision-making process. This study gave him the necessary orientation and set up the base for him and top management to agree on what the company looked like. It also provided the departure point for the planning that followed.

The corporate planner brought us a new and specialized vocabulary. He presented us with a discipline with which management had to clothe its objectives if planning was to be something more than an expensive plaything. As a planner, he met with the usual internal problems. Gradually, however, his professional skills and top management backing (he reported directly to me) won him the confidence of our management team and the cooperation of divisions.

With top management, the director of planning looked at the existing corporate objectives and hammered them out into specific goals that expressed what management really wanted to achieve. Constraints that identified the objectives and the means of achieving them were added. But, more important, these constraints provided a method of measuring progress toward these goals.

An informal study was next made of the company's image in the financial community. It was found that many analysts considered both Univis and the optical industry too small to warrant more than passing attention. It was obvious to us, on the other hand, that our financial performance in terms of growth was outstanding and deserved recognition.

It occurred to the planning director that identifying Univis as a "growth" company would make the financial community pay more attention to us. This seemed reasonable. So we adopted a standard for high annual earnings increases as a corporate goal and explained our business philosophy in the opening paragraphs of the formal five-year corporate plan: "Acknowledging the limitations thereto, it is our contention that over a reasonable period, the single most comprehensive indicator of a public company's performance, though not the only one, is the price of its common stock share."

Our corporate objective followed quite naturally: "Thus, as a reflection of intended long-run operating excellence, our fundamental objective is to maximize owners' common share price."

These decisions cleared the way for our first formal five-year plan, which went into effect in March 1964. Specific programs were spelled out in detail for the first three years. The remaining two years were kept flexible, with product development and acquisitions/mergers in reserve for plugging the gap between what we are doing and what we need to do to reach our goals.

In several significant ways, this and succeeding corporate plans have furnished guides to decision making. They have recognized, for example, the importance of risk, yield, and time factors, and they have provided standards and procedures for appraising alternate uses of assets.

Since risk is inevitable, it is desirable to estimate how much and what kind of risk we will encounter. Is the investment worth the risk? What level of risk is management willing to take to achieve a given yield within the estimated time? We classify the level of risk by referring to standards describing our three risk categories: conservative, normal, and speculative. If we are unhappy with the risk level in an investment situation, we reshuffle time and yield, if possible, to produce a risk level that management is willing to accept.

These standards of risk function as constraints on investment, but not restraints. They are, in effect, a control to help us pick the best investments to fulfill our earnings objectives. Using them, we appraise our activities by product line. Most areas withstand the test; one, in particular, did not. In 1965 we sold the electro-optics division. We found better uses for the assets.

The latest version of our formal five-year corporate plan is oriented toward continuous aggressive expansion in our core industry—ophthalmics. It is another milestone, the beginning of long-range planning at Univis.

In 1955, we had no one devoting full attention to formal planning. Today, our corporate planning department is composed of three professional planners and three service personnel, and it is headed by a company officer.

Univis finished the year 1965 with revenues of $15,513,000 and net earnings of $958,000. In 1966, revenues increased to $16,388,000 and net earnings to $1,005,000. In 1967, the company experienced a strike and subsequent production problems in one of its main plants. As a result, its earnings were affected in the latter part of 1967 and for several months in 1968. Even under these adverse circumstances, however, planning proved its value, for a turn-around was accomplished in 12 months that some people told us would take 3 years. Operations at Univis are back to normal, and plans call for the most sizable gains in both revenues and profits in 1969 that the company has yet experienced.

A Proven Formula
for Acquisition

Harold M. Marko

Triple-A Company Looking for Acquisitions." That's
the ad we ran in *The Wall Street Journal*. It was our first
experience in the acquisitions game; and, frankly, we didn't
know what to expect.

The year was 1958, a bad one for the auto industry and
a bad one for us, too. Ninety percent of our business was in
car-door hinges and other automotive parts. The $78,000
year-end profit wasn't much to show for sales of $5 million.
That poor profit showing made me a very unhappy vice
president of sales. Each generation of management, going

Harold M. Marko is President, Soss Consolidated Inc., Birmingham,
Michigan.

back to the company's beginning in 1909, had seemed content to tie the corporate fortunes to the auto industry's temperamental cycles. But the company obviously couldn't go on that way much longer.

With the approval of the directors, we embarked on an acquisition program. As a result, we have brought in four new divisions, reduced the automobile portion of the business to around 40 percent, raised sales from $5 million to $28 million, and boosted profits from $78,000 to $1.3 million—all in nine years.

Looking back, I believe much of the credit goes to a financial formula we developed for acquiring companies. The formula is fundamentally simple, yet flexible enough to be tailored to special situations. It calls for a cash down payment based on the acquisition's net worth, provisions for sharing the profits with the former owners for the first five years, and a final lump-sum payment based on the acquisition's profit performance. But we didn't perfect the formula until some years later.

Of the 60 replies to our 1958 newspaper ad, all but one came from brokers. The exception was a letter from the treasurer of Newbury Manufacturing Company. He invited us to come down to Talladega, Alabama, to look over Newbury's foundry business.

The company's profits were minimal, but its management was sound and we used iron castings in making hinges. That part of the business by itself would have justified the purchase. But we were more interested in Newbury's license from International Nickel to produce something that was new at the time—ductile iron, a high-grade cross between malleable iron and steel. We felt ductile iron had a great future.

We bought Newbury for $500,000 in cash, eventually sold off the gray-iron part of the business, and concentrated on building up the ductile-iron operation. Soss now had its first division. And in the following year, 1959, profits from the Newbury Division kept Soss from going into the red.

That close call prompted us to straighten out some of our basic corporate problems. For the first time, we thoroughly studied our costs of doing business. We introduced training programs for both management and production people, installed modern labor-saving equipment, and took the first steps toward breaking away from union pacts that tied our wage rates to those of the auto industry.

In 1960, I became president and chief executive officer. A year later I got Soss back on the acquisition track with the purchase of Du-Al Manufacturing Company, makers of farm equipment. The president and sole owner wanted $1,250,000. That was too much for us, even though the company had a history of good earnings. We offered $750,000 as a down payment with this accompanying proposal: Soss would take the first $50,000 in after-tax profits and split the remainder with the owner for ten years or until he received $1,250,000—whichever came first. The owner accepted the offer. (That $50,000 covered principal and interest on the bank loan we took out for the cash down payment.) Result? In its first year as a Soss division,

Du-Al boosted its sales and profits by 50 percent. We paid off the former owner in five and a half years.

The financial formula that we use today grew out of negotiations in 1964 for the purchase of the Mueller Steam Specialty Company, a manufacturer of strainers and pressure-reducing valves. The company's annual sales were approximately $2 million; its profits were good. Two brothers owned and ran the company. Their asking price was $2 million. We were working out the details of the purchase, using our standard ten-year formula, when Congress began a debate on proposed tax legislation to remove installment reporting of income on deals extending beyond five years. That ended the talks for the time being.

We reopened negotiations several weeks later with a new proposal. We offered a $1-million cash down payment with the proviso that we would take the first $85,000 in after-tax profits and split the remainder for five instead of ten years. In addition, we offered to give the brothers, at the end of five years, a lump-sum payment based on $10 for every $1 in after-tax profits that the acquisition earned over a mutually agreed-on base. They agreed. (Incidentally, the proposed tax legislation never became law.)

We used the formula again in 1965 when we purchased The Amprobe Instrument Corporation, manufacturers of electrical testing instruments and the Lampette, a popular high-intensity lamp. In making this acquisition, we were well aware that the formula protects the buyer on the down side. It was just possible that Amprobe's high-intensity lamp business would turn out to be another hula-hoop affair. If it did, profits might slide off. At the same time, our final purchase price would be proportionately lower, and we would still end up paying a reasonable price for Amprobe's highly profitable instrument-manufacturing business.

The formula offers advantages to the seller, too. As the profitability of his former company increases in the five years after acquisition, so does his final selling price. The former owner of Amprobe, for example, accepted $1,460,000 down and a split of the profits over $125,000. Figuring in a lump-sum payment based on continued good earnings, he has the opportunity to make $4 million on the sale of his company. He was asking $3 million.

Using profitability as a major factor in determining the final selling price is an incentive for the seller to become part of the new management and contribute his talents to the company's growth. We welcome this arrangement, since we want capable and experienced managers to stay on. The former owner of Newbury wanted to sell out and retire. He did. The Du-Al management stayed on and prospered. The company, formerly No. 2 in its field, is now the industry leader. The two brothers who sold us Mueller Steam are now that division's president and vice president, and we hope they stay on beyond their five-year contracts.

The formula also keeps the seller "honest." We don't ask ourselves why a man wants to sell his company. We do ask ourselves whether there are reasons he doesn't want us to know about. His acceptance of the formula's flexible payment provisions is insurance against any skeletons in the corporate closet—a latent labor problem, an impending loss of a major customer, basically defective products. In addition, we ask him to guarantee—under penalty of returning payment—that his balance sheets are correct.

The buyer who uses the formula has his problems, too. If the new acquisition grows faster than expected, he can wind up paying more for the company than he really wanted to. If the buyer sells an acquisition that has gone bad, he may discover when he makes his next acquisition move that his company's reputation has been damaged. Fortunately, we have not been faced with these situations. We hope we never will be. We substantially reduce the likelihood of a bad choice by being reasonably sure of what we're looking for in the first place. We seek companies that have

- Manufacturing technology related to our own, using metalworking as a common denominator.
- Widespread distribution of product. No one customer should account for more than 15 percent of the volume.
- A history of increasing sales and profits in a growth area.
- Minimum sales of $2 million with after-tax profits of at least 5 percent. The exception is a company with a low-earnings situation that is quickly correctable.
- Good, or potentially good, management that is capable of running the acquisition if the former owner/

manager should leave. Key people should be adaptable and willing to learn new techniques to improve company performance.

To date, we have joined acquisitions to the company as divisions operating on the profit-center concept. They have their own product lines and markets, but all basic management policies and financial controls are centralized in corporate headquarters. Division presidents report directly to me. Division vice presidents report to their corporate counterparts. Computers give us a day-by-day accounting of each division's sales, disbursements, and other key operating factors. And corporate management learns what the division's problems are and how they are being handled by reading the uncensored minutes of the weekly division staff meeting.

I operate on the theory that corporate management will never know the business as well as division people, but we are always ready with financial resources and the personnel to help divisions improve their operations. We can, for example, help divisions set up data processing, production and process engineering systems, marketing and sales analysis, and cost-accounting controls. However, we move only at a division's request—a point we guarantee in writing in the acquisition agreement.

There is no charge to divisions for the use of corporate resources for equipment or working capital. And there is no charge for the salaries of technical or administrative people we lend them unless—by mutual consent—they stay on in the division for some length of time. Divisions are billed only for the travel, hotel, and telephone expenses for corporate people on loan.

Most of our acquired companies had never operated with up-to-date methods and controls. Most of them, in fact, were run pretty much by the seat of the pants. Even then, they were operating profitably. I'm sure some holdover division managers ask themselves at times what the old company's profits might have been if modern management practices had been used.

Here is the Soss acquisition formula as we have refined it:

1. A cash down payment roughly equal to the net worth of the acquisition.
2. A performance bonus that calls for
   - *Soss to retain from profits after taxes for the first five years an amount equal to 10 percent of the down payment. (This is, so to speak, a return on down-payment investment.)*
   - *Soss and the seller of the acquired company to split the remaining profits on a 50–50 basis.*
3. A final payment to bring the total purchase price to an amount equal to ten times the increase in profits over a mutually agreed-on profit base averaged over five years.

Assume, for example, that a company has a net worth of $500,000, an average annual profit base of $100,000, and an average annual after-tax profit of $200,000 for the first five years. Since the average annual profit for the first five years has exceeded the mutually agreed-on profit base by $100,000, Soss is committed to paying $1 million (10 × $100,000) as the total cost of the acquisition.

The following payments would have been made under the purchase agreement by the end of the five-year period:

▪ A *down payment of*	$ 500,000
▪ *Five profit-sharing payments of $75,- 000 each, based on a 50–50 split of $150,000 ($200,000 profit minus $50,000 retained by Soss)*	375,000
▪ *Lump-sum or final payment at the end of the five-year period to make up the difference between these two payments combined and the com- mitted purchase price for the acqui- sition, or $1 million*	125,000
Total cost of acquisition	$1,000,000

I expect that we will make some changes in the acquisition formula in the years ahead. But we do not plan to change the basic philosophy that calls for the formula to serve the best interests of both the buyer and the seller. Over the long run, this is a fundamentally sound and profitable basis for successful acquisition programs.

The Inexorable Pressure
of Technology

David Sarnoff

Sweeping changes in American business since World War
II have brought unprecedented challenges to the art of
management. Technology and growth, costs and competition have placed a new premium on judgment and accuracy
in decision making.

It used to be said that a man who was right 51 percent
of the time was a good executive. Today, there is no room
for so wide a tolerance of error. Our society and the corporations that serve it have become too large and too complex. A mistake in one strategic business decision is likely to

David Sarnoff is Chairman of the Board, RCA, New York City. He
is a former President of RCA.

be so costly that the man who makes it will probably never be given a second opportunity.

The mounting burden of responsibility has been the reason in large part for the extraordinary growth of electronic systems that assemble, organize, transmit, and display virtually unlimited quantities of meaningful intelligence for management decision. They operate so swiftly that the information produced is almost instantly available. Related advances have made it possible to use the information to stimulate and study the probable consequences of such decisions in the production and marketing areas.

The pace of progress in management electronics is so rapid that tomorrow's technology will operate far beyond the limits of the most advanced concepts in use today. Computers soon will respond to any form of instruction— written, printed, oral, or visual. Through high-capacity satellite, transistorized cable, and microwave communications, they will exchange data in enormous volume over any global distance. Computer memories will become larger and faster, to the point where they will store trillions of bits of information for retrieval in billionths of a second. Advances in machine logic and electronic circuitry will lead to new types of systems that learn from experience and adapt themselves to new functions.

Within the next decade, these developments will equip management with a total information system that will reach into all areas of business, no matter how large, how diverse, or how far-flung its facilities. The manager will have instant access to information that relates directly to all parts of his enterprise and to external conditions which may affect his operation. This information will span the total spectrum by its ability to recall the past, to reflect upon the present, and to estimate the future.

As progress quickens in the development of larger and more effective information storage and retrieval systems, it will be possible to place all corporate information in a central data bank. This will be linked to all units of the enterprise, so that significant business changes are reflected at a single point. The data bank will become a store of dynamic information that can monitor operations and reveal how closely performance is matching objectives.

A total management information system will not only help management with the assessment of variable factors and the consideration of long-range problems, it will introduce far greater flexibility and responsiveness at all levels in day-to-day affairs.

In the future, unified planning will be possible to an extent never before attainable. With a comprehensive and up-to-the-minute view of the enterprise at many levels, there may be a recentralization of control in industries which are physically decentralized in location and organization. Moreover, electronic files for permanent storage and video devices for instant data retrieval and display will radically reduce the accumulation of paperwork.

But, while the prospect is bright for better information and more sophisticated management techniques, it is vital to recognize that there are inherent limitations in any man-made system. Machines cannot substitute for human intelligence and intuition or for the ultimate responsibilities of management. As the manager gains access to more comprehensive information and evaluation, a greater value is placed upon his own understanding and judgment. Electronics can and will sharpen his capabilities, but there will always be the point beyond which he is entirely on his own.

I see the ultimate responsibility of the manager as the one constant in an electronic revolution. The human decision will always be the yardstick of executive management. But the yardstick tomorrow will be calibrated more precisely than ever before. This is the challenge as well as the opportunity for managerial talent.

Are Your Management Habits
and Rituals Outmoded?

Louis B. Lundborg

IN THOSE dark, early days of World War II, the British
were forced to use every piece of armament and every bit of
manpower, no matter how outdated the equipment or, for
that matter, the man. One make of gun, for example, had a
history that stretched back to the premechanized days of
the Boer War. Hitched to trucks instead of horses, these
guns served as mobile coastal defense units.

A time-and-motion expert was called in to suggest ways
to step up the rate of fire. He took slow-motion pictures of

LOUIS B. LUNDBORG is Chairman of the Board and Executive Officer
(Southern Division), Bank of America National Trust and Savings Association, in Los Angeles.

the elderly Home Defense gun crews going through the loading, aiming, and firing procedures. When he projected the pictures, he noticed something that mystified him. A moment before firing, two members of the crew stopped and stood at attention for the three-second interval during which the gun was actually fired. The expert showed the film to an ancient colonel of artillery and asked him to explain the puzzling behavior of the two men. The colonel was equally puzzled at first and asked to see the film again. This time, when the two men snapped to attention, the colonel smacked his hands together and exclaimed, "I have it! They're holding the horses!"

Some men protect themselves from the shock of change by continuing familiar habits and rituals even if they are meaningless in new situations. But old habits, as every chief executive knows, are hard to break. How many times do we think in clichés? How many times do we assume that if we do everything just as we've always done it before, we will be doing it the best way possible? We are confident that what goes up must come down. Then one day someone launches a satellite. How often do we think that, if all is quiet, we must be doing our job? We might also be dead.

For some years now there has been on the market an engaging little toy—a small black box with a lever on top. When the lever is moved to one side, the box begins to emit a variety of clicking, whirring, and grinding noises. Then slowly the lid rises. A hand inches out and pushes the lever back to the starting position, then recedes into the box as the lid closes.

There is a great deal of little-black-boxism in every area of management. In many companies, action follows only a specific stimulus, such as a customer complaint or a chewing-out from the boss. But management is much more challenging and exciting than this black-box behavior—which is essentially reacting instead of acting. And management that merely reacts can maintain neither itself nor its company in an era such as ours when all factors in our business environment are changing so rapidly.

One such factor is population. It is growing and changing at an unprecedented rate. It is younger: Between 1960 and 1970, the median age of our population will have dropped seven or eight years, the largest recorded drop in population statistics. And this young, growing population is better educated. Fifty percent of the young men and 40 percent of the girls of college age are in college. Most of them live in that urban phenomenon we call megalopolis. They were born into a fast-changing world and have acquired some of the adaptive tools of survival. Twenty years of formal education is not at all unusual among these people. Many specialize in two or even three technical fields.

This single change factor—population—is seething with implications for our organizations. As the world becomes more complex, as the needs of customers become more specialized, so our institutions must become more complex, more highly specialized. We require the services of intelligent, well-educated young people. We need all types of specialized people with specialized knowledge and skills.

We need their help in strengthening our institutions to meet the future which will be made by others like them.

To react to these facts defensively, or simply to ignore them, is just another case of holding the horses. To say they are unimportant is to deny that the age-center of gravity in our society is shifting downward. The values and attitudes that will soon be the dominant ones in America will be those of a generation that has an education and set of experiences very different from our own.

This new breed of young people will make different demands on us, both as customers and as employees. Gearing ourselves to meet the challenge will not be an easy task. But, easy or not, we must begin now to redefine the relationship between ourselves and our managers and the young people who will one day succeed us.

To attract young people to our companies, and to hold them, we must present a corporate environment that is responsive to their needs. This will involve some adjustments on our part. For centuries, many of our businesses have operated under an apprenticeship system; many of us in top management today are products of that system. But young people are impatient. They want to prove that their years of education have not been wasted. They want responsibility. They want opportunity. And they want it now.

Many of us tend to sneer at those who are different from us. At one time or another, we have all passed judgment on young executives with phrases such as "He's too pushy," "He's in too much of a hurry," or "I guess he's all right, but he certainly is a strange fellow." We must get over this sneer syndrome. Many different talents and many types of people are needed to keep our organizations young and alive. The effective executive knows how to harness the specialized talents of others. Each of us as chief executive must see that his bright young people are challenged.

This does not require that corporate controls be turned over to a younger, less experienced, or more impetuous group. Gray hair is not an indication of obsolescence, but neither is it a guarantee of wisdom. I do not imply that this new wave of youth will have all the answers. Nor do I boast a perfect understanding of, or comfortable acquiescence to, some of the things young people do nowadays. But we must confront, not confound, the tide of youth. We must explore, not deplore.

I believe there are rules that will help our organizations not only to survive but to flourish in this world of change. The first and perhaps primary rule is to recognize what business we are in. IBM began to navigate with a clear vision that placed it years ahead of its competitors when top management realized the company was in the business of processing information, not making office machines. Xerox used to be in the copying-machine business. Now it sees itself in the business of making information and knowledge broadly and quickly available to great numbers of people everywhere. In the same way, my own organization is not simply in the business of attracting deposits and making loans. It is a merchandiser of financial services, help, and advice. It is in the business of moving money from idle to productive use. It is in the business of helping individuals, communities, entire regions to a better way of life.

Second, management must be tough-minded and see things as they are. We must have people with courage to probe and question established beliefs. Third, we must have men who are willing to hold unpopular opinions; men who will speak out. Great deeds are born through creative tension and forged on the anvil of argument and dissent.

Fourth, we must be profit-oriented. Every project, every expenditure, every use of company time or money must be directed toward profit. We must ruthlessly judge every activity for its contribution to corporate objectives—both short- and long-term.

Fifth, we must study, recognize, and understand social change. If we do not plan for change, we will be caught in an endless series of profitless, haphazard rear-guard actions with disastrous consequences for our companies.

Not everyone should be expected to play an Olympian role in engineering change. Only a small number of people in any society or any organization have the inspiration, vision, and genius to be true innovators. But there are things that every one of us can do—and, I might add, profit from. As chief executives, we must welcome, understand, and work with change. Grousing about the good old days only leads to hard feelings.

To utilize change profitably we need imagination, education, and experience. Each quality, by itself, is worth very little. Experience, for example, depends on what we do with it. There is a vast difference between 15 years of experience and one year of experience repeated 15 times.

Experience can be a steppingstone to future achievement, or it can be a prison. If you doubt that experience can be a prison, ask yourself this: Why didn't a telegraph company invent the telephone? Or why didn't a silk manufacturer develop nylon? Why didn't a buggy manufacturer create the automobile? Why didn't the railroads pioneer the airplane?

Successful organizations combine wisdom and insight gained from experience with the vigor, enthusiasm, and freshness of viewpoint associated with youth. The new virtues blend—they don't clash—with the old. We pass on to our younger associates an ability to avoid past pitfalls. They bring us, in return, new perspectives and new tools for solving old problems.

A company that combines the old and the new is mature in judgment and young at heart. It is deliberate and sure-footed while confident and bold. Change is a way of life, not an obstruction. And in such a company change makes the prospects for success, well into the future, great indeed.

Ordeal by Computer:
Being Your Own Programmer

David R. Fairbairn

THE COMPUTER company's survey of our data processing needs was right out of the rule book. It recommended that we lease a relatively simple computer, design the system to handle routine accounting functions, and recruit a programmer to set up the system and keep it running. So that I would know what was going on, I was to take a two-week orientation course.

The recommendations seemed to be sound and sensible, but I had my doubts. To begin with, we had made our

DAVID R. FAIRBAIRN is Marketing Director of Guinness Overseas Limited, London. He was formerly President, The Guinness-Harp Corporation, Long Island City, New York.

own study and come to the somewhat heretical conclusion that marketing should have top priority in data processing. Accounting would be second in line. This made more sense to us, since Guinness-Harp is a marketing and distributing company, the American arm of the worldwide Guinness brewing organization based in Dublin.

In 1964, a proposal to put in EDP had been rejected. "Too expensive" was the verdict. "Hold off." Two years later, in 1966, we got the go-ahead to install the computer. At the same time, we proposed a new marketing plan that called for directed selling techniques, flexible sales territories, and a reorganized sales force that could be shifted to meet changing sales patterns in the imported beer market. We had four brands, sold nationally. Two were Guinness products: Guinness stout, a dark malt beer; and Harp, a light lager. We also handled two other European brands: Bass ale from England and Amstel beer from Holland. In addition, we distributed other domestic and imported brands in New York, delivering to the retailer in our own trucks.

The New York metropolitan area accounted for close to one-third of all imported beer sold in the United States. This was the prime market. It was also the battleground for 302 imported brands. The plan was to increase our share of the market by capitalizing on the specialized character of our products.

To carry out the plan, we needed detailed sales and marketing data and a program of administrative and budgetary controls. We had been compiling information on our 10,000 metropolitan area accounts on hand-kept records, but it was a cumbersome and complicated operation. We needed the computer's ability to quickly digest and extract information to develop the new marketing plan and make it workable.

The suggested equipment, an IBM 402, was a good choice. It was a first-generation, card-stored system that could be readily upgraded to more sophisticated equipment. We placed the order in late 1966. Delivery was scheduled for June 1967. In the meantime, we began transferring the information from the hand-kept records to punch cards.

I deferred the decision to recruit a staff programmer until I had picked up a working knowledge of the computer's language. I would be even better qualified to pick a programmer, I reasoned, if I had complete command of the language, especially the programmer's jargon. So instead of the two-week orientation session, I signed on for the full programming course: four hours a night for four days a week for four months. I reserved the weekends for homework.

The programmer, I discovered, has two primary roles. First, he knows where to go for information, what to do with it, and where to print it out. Second, he has the quasi-mechanical job of "wiring" the program into the computer, much as a switchboard operator plugs in telephone lines. In all cases, he follows the priorities set by management on data to be fed in and printed out. Since I would be issuing the priorities, and since I already knew where to go for the data, I decided halfway through the course that I might as well program the computer myself. This was welcome news back at the office. At least the threatened changes would be at the hands of an insider. We were all learning together now.

In the early months of 1967, we began a series of employee meetings to explain how the computer worked and what we planned to do with it. Rather than bring in experienced computer operators who would have to be taught our marketing procedures, we trained our office staff to run the computer. (I believe the transition to EDP was quick and free of major problems because of this decision.) At the same time, our marketing vice president was teaching the concepts of market planning to the eight district managers who handled our national distribution through hundreds of wholesale outlets. These men soon learned a new marketing language built around such terms as "situa· tion analysis," "strategy," "sales forecasts," "budget requests," and "depletion reports."

The computer arrived in June 1967, right on schedule. The initial input was the 10,000 previously punched cards with data on sales by brand, income level and ethnic characteristics of consumers, frequency of purchase, location and type of account (restaurant, hotel, supermarket, bar), salesman, number of items sold, product mix on the delivery truck, and the account area as identified in government census tables.

Using the first data analysis, we redrew the sales territories and set sales quotas for the coming year. At the same time, we reorganized the sales force. The first step was to dissolve the unionized sales force and to reform it as a nonunion operation which would not be restricted to prescribed territories. Instead of paying our salesmen on a commission basis, we put the 18-man sales force on salary with a graduated bonus plan based on results over sales quotas. Paying commissions, I had observed, encouraged the lone-wolf approach to selling. Our goal was to create a sales force that would work together and respond quickly to market changes. Flexibility was the key factor. We wanted the prerogative of redrawing territories and reassigning salesmen if necessary. All this was possible because of the computer's ability to keep track of transactions and to extract and print out sales forecasts, quotas, and budget variances on command.

What did we learn from the initial sales analysis? First of all, the conclusions of an earlier study were strengthened. Despite the Irish background of Guinness stout and Harp beer, sales in New York's Irish neighborhoods were not significantly higher than in mixed white areas. This was a surprise. Better than one-third of Guinness sales were in Negro areas with strong West Indian influences. This was no surprise. Around the world, stout is associated with masculinity and strength, important values in less developed societies. More than half of all sales were off-premise. This conformed to domestic sales patterns, but differed from the patterns of most imported beers. Also, Guinness stout didn't have a strong snob appeal.

As a result, our advertising went from class to mass. We abandoned *The New Yorker, The New York Times Sun-*

day Magazine, and *Time.* We went instead to *The New York Daily News,* subway advertising, and radio. Except for point-of-sale and special holiday promotions, we didn't push the Irish heritage of Guinness products. Once we had learned who was buying our products and where, and could aim our marketing resources in the right direction, sales of Guinness stout alone rose 25 percent in a 12-month period.

We also learned that people need time to adjust to the computer. Despite my many hours of personal contact with the relatively small number of people directly involved, it took four months for the staff to become enthusiastic EDP supporters. People are accustomed to the printed word, but most of them pull back at the sight of figures and strange coded symbols. If there's a problem, they blame it on the alien machine. People, however, make the mistakes, and we had our share of problems in the early months. Of the 10,000 cards processed in the first input, 1,500 cards, or 15 percent, had to be amended.

Even more frustrating is the computer's demand for precise information to be prepared in a systematic manner. We had to tighten up our system for reporting depletion and inventory and for shipments and billings. Everyone from clerk to executive re-examined his working procedures and adjusted them to the new demands. It was a painful experience in some cases, but also productive. With better control over their jobs, people began to feel that they were in command of the machine, and not the other way around.

In late 1967, we brought the computer-based reporting and control system down to individual salesmen. We asked them to prepare route books listing their accounts in the order in which they called on them, giving the day and approximate time during the two-week cycle. Sales data are updated every two weeks, thus giving each salesman a current picture of what he *should* be doing, what he *is* doing, and where he is *off target*. Basically, that's all he needs to know. The route book, in turn, tells us whether the salesman is doing his job effectively and whether he is directing his efforts where sales potential is greatest. And that's what we need to know.

We scheduled three weeks for the preparation of route books. We were too optimistic—it took months. Once again, there was resistance to planning and a fear that the book was to be written by machine. Each salesman, I said, determines the order in which he will call on accounts; the computer merely follows instructions. People listened, but some of them evidently didn't hear. They seemed to be paralyzed by fear of the print-out.

The first computerized route books were issued in March amid mild hysteria that quickly quieted to uneasiness as salesmen took them for shakedown cruises in their territories. It was still not a perfected system, but it was improving steadily. Salesmen and supervisors met every afternoon at four to discuss the route reports and to clear up any individual problems. And from time to time I sat in as programmer and systems analyst, looking for ways to improve the procedures and to increase the route book's effectiveness as a sales tool.

Working alongside the salesmen was a special five-man task force charged with opening new accounts and with boosting sales in existing outlets. These marketing missionaries looked for gaps between territories and helped salesmen spot accounts that were likely prospects to take on our other products. Sometimes they stepped in to help the salesman clinch the sale. In every case, credit for the new account or the sales increase went to the salesman. The missionary's good deeds were on straight salary.

The emphasis, as the marketing plan came up for review and territories were reshaped in accordance with new data, would always be on directing our resources toward the potentially most profitable areas. This message was being carried to our wholesale distributors by district managers who operated their districts as profit centers. We wanted to convince these wholesalers, many of them small businessmen, that they could step up their sales and their profits by adopting the new marketing principles. Our district managers would be working with them on developing sales forecasts and budgets, market analyses, and depletion and inventory controls.

The preparation of trend analysis and cumulative reporting on an account-by-account basis that would enable us to use exception reporting more effectively was a project that demanded greater computer capacity and more sophisticated equipment. To this end, an IBM 360/20 computer would eventually make its debut. Preliminary programming was already under way, and a reception committee was being trained in the greatly simplified and improved RPG computer language.

A key man on the reception committee would be the financial controller. He was waiting patiently to put the accounting function on the computer. He might be surprised at first to find Clancy's bar identified as 121H27, but an idea soon catches on. Even Clancy doesn't mind sharing the billing with a number. His sales and his profits have never been better, thanks to our computer.

Happy Go Modern!

Abraham Goodman

In Berkshire Apparel's headquarters in the Boston suburb of Malden, a visitor to the reception area can look through a glass wall and see the computers hard at work. We designed it that way for a purpose.

People who know the company or anything about the women's wear industry (not unjustifiably called "the rag business") will appreciate the significance of seeing computers first, dresses second. For, like so many companies in its industry, Berkshire Apparel had been run through the years largely on hunches. Now Berkshire has gone modern, courtesy of computers.

ABRAHAM GOODMAN has been President and Chairman of the Board, Berkshire Apparel Corporation, Malden, Massachusetts.

As for me, the company founder, I went modern, too. And I became a better and a happier president for it. After seven years' experience in developing a sophisticated computer program that began with a now primitive tab system, I could look back on precomputer days with respect for what we had tried to do and a sense of relief that they were at last part of the past.

I used to wrestle for days with figures that my assistants had compiled after thumbing through stacks of orders and production tickets. I had to know how many garments of each style were made and what was selling, what new fabrics to buy and what to cut to meet demand. Sometimes I waited a week for figures. Once, in a fit of frustration, I switched accountants simply because I couldn't bear the waiting.

Around 1958, Berkshire was stalled on a sales plateau of $5 to $6 million a year. We had no clear-cut program for growth, working virtually from line to line, following the whims of styles and seasons. Part of our problem was obvious: We couldn't get up-to-date information fast enough to beat out competition. It took a week to tabulate orders and plan the purchase of fabrics—too long in a business where a season lasts only eight to ten weeks. Obviously, we had to speed up the flow of paperwork.

Our treasurer suggested electronic data processing. Before joining our company, he had been our accountant. He was also servicing a baby products manufacturer which had computerized. Since no one at Berkshire knew anything about EDP, he suggested hiring the specialist who had set up that company's program. And so, in 1959, that is what we did.

We installed the first EDP tabulating unit that year, and soon learned the first of many lessons to come. We had hoped that this equipment would cut down on administrative costs by replacing half of our main office staff. We quickly abandoned that notion as personnel added staff to handle all the new and exciting information that early-model computer was delivering—and the many problems it was uncovering.

In one case, we found 250 accounts were not being properly covered; so we added more salesmen. In another, it became apparent that our plants were not operating at profitable levels throughout the year, particularly during November and December. Using the computer, we planned workloads a year ahead and increased plant efficiency.

Not surprisingly, executives who at first took a show-me attitude toward computers were quickly won over. Typical was the production vice president, whose enthusiasm grew as fast as plant productivity. For myself, I had been a rooter all along, although I confess there were times I became uneasy over information being uncovered. I now know what they mean when they say ignorance is bliss.

Some old-timers saw computerization as a threat; some middle management people weren't very happy, either. "This isn't going to last long," said our head bookkeeper. She bucked our data processing program for a year. Finally we let her go.

Then we suddenly discovered we had problems with our salesmen. Consider the case of a man we'll call Joe—our biggest commission earner. His territory covered seven states. Data from the computer revealed that Joe was not getting all the potential from his area, even though his annual sales had climbed to $600,000. So we divided his territory, along with the territories of all the other salesmen, to create more efficient sales areas. At this point Joe, who had worked on a guaranteed $42,000 a year for two years, resigned angrily. He felt his integrity had been challenged by a machine. How wrong he was! Joe's territory that once produced $600,000 annual sales is today covered by seven salesmen who bring in $2,800,000.

Hardest hit were the older salesmen who were either unwilling or unable to change. "You have no right to do this to us," said one. "I can't understand why you're not satisfied," complained another. And so, out of 17 salesmen who were with Berkshire B.C. (Before Computers), only four remained with the firm. Salesmen working the new territories find their sales are up and expenses down, and their families are happier because they spend less time on the road.

Speed, we discovered, is one of the computer's greatest contributions to Berkshire's decision-making process. Not long ago, one of the executives proposed that we buy a company doing $3.5 million in annual sales. The proposal made good sense, since we were broadening our product line. The company's management produced records that, while incomplete, looked very good. But, when the data were fed into our computer bank, by now considerably more advanced and sophisticated than our first units, we were stunned by the electronic analysis of the company's finances. I'm sure that company's management had no idea of its actual cost of doing business. We turned down the offer to buy—fast. The computer once again had saved us from what might have been a serious mistake.

While dollar savings attributable directly to computers are difficult to document, there are some blue ribbons to show. We had planned to break even on our computer-equipment investment around the same time that sales hit $9 million. Our target was the end of 1963. Actually, we reached both goals 18 months earlier, in June 1962. And, while sales have since risen, the ratio of administrative costs to sales has remained constant.

Although the computer cannot program intuition, it has replaced guesswork in keeping tab on orders by colors and sizes. Result: Fewer markdowns at the end of the season; more profits. Cost figures now come in fast enough to help price products more realistically. And the computer sends up a red flag whenever costs on a given garment line start to get out of line or when it looks as though sales might be outdistancing production.

But the biggest blessing has been the Retail Unit Control System (RUC), devised by the company's executive vice president and the controller. For good reasons, the system has attracted industrywide attention. RUC assures retailers they will always have Berkshire stock on hand while their inventories are kept to a minimum.

Working with the retailer's own records of past sales performance, Berkshire programs his projected sales for the year by unit and season, sets up a stock plan tailored to his sales needs, and schedules deliveries so stores will always have garments on the racks to meet customer demands. The system requires two minutes for the computer to assemble the store's statistics, a minute or so for a girl to keypunch the data, and 17 seconds for the computer to run off the year's sales program.

The computer has also helped uncover problems in the shipping room. On one occasion we sent through an order to ship 1,500 units of a certain item. There should have been no problem; we had 1,500 units in stock. But the computer soon discovered that only 1,000 units had been shipped. What had happened to the other 500? The shipping room foreman, it turned out, liked to cut down on packing by making large shipments. So he shipped the 1,000 units and held the remaining 500 to be packed in with the next large order for that store. Thanks to the computer, we caught the mistake and rushed the remaining stock to the store just in time for the height of the season. As for the foreman, he's now working in another department.

My faith in the computer's ability to spot trouble quickly helped me loosen my grip on operations. I used to be president, head salesman, production chief, promotion director, materials buyer, and stylist. But, thanks to the computer, Berkshire stopped being a one-man show. As a result, I could spend twice as much time working with stylists in New York, planning for next season's numbers. And styling at Berkshire is a chief-executive function.

Before EDP, I used to work alone a great deal, partly because I didn't have the organization I needed, partly because I couldn't get information fast enough to check the performance of my executives and thus build up my confidence in them. While I still was inclined to work closely with department heads, I no longer held—or bound —their hands. We worked as a team, contrary to the usual practice in most of our industry. I still carried the deciding vote, but I listened to my four top men, I respected their views, and they knew it.

At least three-quarters of the paperwork that used to cross my desk vanished, and I didn't miss it. I saw a great deal more significant information on much less paper. In terms of the entire company, however, we were getting five times more paper than we ever saw before, and I'm not convinced that this sort of thing should be happening.

I used to think that mechanized information retrieval would replace good old-fashioned business acumen. I don't think so now. The computer can tell us what women went for last season, but it can't predict next season's winners. What it does is help us make some pretty good decisions by taking past reactions to fabrics and patterns and interpreting them in the light of what we know about the business. This is using the computer creatively.

Looking back, I'm convinced that one of the biggest problems in computerization is people. If I could relive my years of electronic data processing, I would start out by showing my people how computers work in other companies. Instead of trying to talk up our system, I would want them to talk to others who have been converted. And, once EDP is installed, I would ask them to keep giving us suggestions on how to improve the computer's effectiveness within their departments.

This is the kind of hindsight that produced these guidelines for setting up an EDP system:

1. Find the right specialist to head up the system and make him part of your top management team. Be sure he knows all your problems and your plans for the future.
2. Make improved long-range efficiency rather than short-range savings your objective.
3. Follow established procedures wherever you can to lessen the pain of human adjustment. Invoice forms, for example, should look as much as possible like the pre-EDP invoice forms.
4. Avoid complicated procedures that frighten people. New procedures are more readily accepted if done piecemeal, then pulled together later.
5. Tailor the system to the people who must work with it.
6. Beware of too much information. Select only those reports that you really need and that people have time and ability to handle. If you give them more than they can absorb, they're likely not to look at anything.

7. Don't expect maximum efficiency overnight. As confidence and understanding grow, improvements will follow.
8. Above all, don't despair about today's problem. The computer may turn up an even bigger one tomorrow.

Today's Two-Pronged Challenge

Rudolph A. Peterson

As PROBLEMS and pressures affecting our economy at all levels daily become more complex, there is a continually growing need for American businessmen to apply their managerial capabilities to the area of public affairs.

For the first time in history, government at all levels has acknowledged that it cannot cope unilaterally with such contemporary problems as air and water pollution, housing, urban development, mass transit, and racial unrest—to say nothing of the deepening fiscal difficulties which beset our nation.

RUDOLPH A. PETERSON is President and Chief Executive Officer, Bank of America National Trust and Savings Association, San Francisco.

Indeed, no single entity can handle these problems. They demand the best minds of our generation from all fields. Only a task force that brings together the most imaginative and realistic viewpoints from business, governmental, educational, and institutional worlds can begin to grapple with the issues of the day. In this framework, it is the obligation of business to participate and involve itself deeply with all the sectors of the nation. Lip service will not solve problems. Indeed, it will only further aggravate them.

This presents business with a two-pronged challenge— our social and economic responsibilities to the nation and our responsibility to our companies. The key to our nation's economic growth and health is found in that dynamic word—profit. Only the corporation that is strong and healthy can afford to divert a significant portion of its efforts and earnings to improving our environment and the lives of our citizens. The chief executive who forgets this fact in his zeal for service accomplishes nothing.

We must achieve a delicate balance. We must involve ourselves meaningfully in the issues of the day, because to ignore them at this stage in history is to invite doom. We must, at the same time, tend to our own house with great care, because to overlook our corporate vitality is to undermine our nation's economic well-being. It is, therefore, our obligation to seek a *real* partnership with government in which businesses can continue to make normal profits for taking normal risks while government accepts major responsibility for nonnormal or nonmarket risks. In this partnership, our counsel should be heard and considered on a wide range of matters. We should not merely be consulted when a consensus is sought. We must speak out on economic policies and trends that we feel are unwise or unsound. We must speak out for greater fiscal responsibility at home and abroad. In both cases, we have the information and the capability to evaluate these matters much more realistically than the average citizen.

While there is little question of the basic strength and productive muscle of our national economy, there is also little question that we have problems. Full employment itself has brought new problems. Domestic prices and wages are increasing more rapidly than is healthy, and the epidemic of strikes across the nation indicates that this trend may continue. The deficit in our balance of payments has become much too dangerous to be brushed aside as simply a continuing sore spot. The deficit in our Federal budget is putting severe strains on domestic financial markets. Restrictive monetary policies have pushed up interest rates and sharply reduced the supply of credit available to certain sectors of our economy.

Private enterprise can and must play a new and more aggressive role in the social and economic life of the nation. We may have to insist upon a key part in the development of the great projects that must be undertaken. We should, as an initial step, demand that priorities in spending at home and abroad be set. This is the way we run our companies. We should urge that our governmental bodies be run in this way as well. The time has never been more favorable.

In short, businessmen are going to be called upon more and more to use all their skills and resources to solve local, national, and international problems. At the same time, we will be facing greater competitive and earning pressures. Will we be equal to the task? I think so. American business today is proving itself to be the most dynamic and innovative element in world society. We have a responsibility to employ that creativity for the public, but we must not lose sight of our basic responsibility to our companies.

Communications Chief:
A Job for the President

W. F. Rockwell, Jr.

COMMUNICATIONS has become a vital function of modern industry. It can no longer take a secondary position in the corporate scheme of things; nor can it be relegated exclusively to the attention of staff specialists.

The merits of an effective communications program in even the smallest company are no longer debatable. Good corporate communications produces definitely measurable results in terms such as goodwill within the community, understanding among employees, and acceptance from customers and prospects.

W. F. ROCKWELL, JR., is Chairman of the Board, North American Rockwell Corporation, and formerly President and Chief Executive Officer of Rockwell-Standard Corporation.

Communications, whether internal or external, is the corporate voice. Therefore, it falls to the president to play a dominant role in shaping and breathing life into his company's communications policy. And the president's job doesn't end with policy formulation. He should be actively and continually concerned with *how* it's said, *when* it's said, *where* it's said. He becomes, then, the communications chief of his company.

The president's acceptance of the role of communications chief immediately raises the question, "How much should we communicate?" And again the president must necessarily play the dominant role in formulating company policy. This isn't to say it should be an ivory-tower decision; just the opposite. But the question of how much to communicate is so basic to any communications program that the views of the president are key factors in framing a policy.

If the president favors a policy of rather complete disclosure of business information, he must make his feelings known to his staff specialists in communications or to his public relations agency—or to both. The tendency at the second or third levels of management is, in most companies, to take the conservative approach as a hedge against incurring the chief executive's displeasure by disclosing too much.

Consider the old parlor game where a message is whispered into the ear of one person who then repeats it to the next—and so on until everyone in the room has heard it. The last person then stands and repeats the message aloud. Seldom does the final statement resemble the initial one.

And the more people are involved, the more garbled the message becomes. This is the way it is with presidential communications. As more and more staff and agency personnel "interpret" the president's comments, those comments become progressively watered down or distorted until, in the end, they are often bland, meaningless, or—worst of all—incorrect. For this reason, it is necessary for the president to play an active role in communications—a role that has him communicating directly and frequently with those who actually disseminate the corporation's communications.

Even if the president leans toward minimum disclosure of operating data, he should make this known at the outset so his staff and agency communications experts can frame a program accordingly.

Beyond the obvious benefits of having the president establish the company's communications philosophy, there's a psychological advantage in having the president personally involved. The sad history of too many corporate communications programs is that they start with a great flurry; large supplies of attractive, specially designed letterheads are ordered; and, long before the initial supply is exhausted, the communications program withers away. This is unlikely to happen if everyone knows from the outset that the communications program is a personal project of the president.

This, of course, is not to suggest deception or the use of the president's office for an activity that does not deserve his attention. An *effective*, serious communications program certainly merits the continuing attention of the president. Anything less deserves the attention and interest of neither the president nor the employees to whom it is directed and, therefore, should never be started.

Answering the question of how much to communicate involves the weighing of varying shades of gray in addition to the routine blacks and whites. In other words, there cannot be absolute or total disclosure, just as there should not be a refusal to disclose anything.

In our company we feel that the results of a communications program will normally be in direct proportion to the degree of disclosure. To be successful communicators we must personally involve the recipients, and this is best done by communicating information of real interest and value. Accordingly, we have adopted a policy of near-total disclosure.

Much of the information we disclose would, in most firms, probably be restricted to the executive board or board of directors. We apply the restricted-information policy in only two places: when discussing acquisitions still in the negotiating stage and when disclosing product-by-product profitability.

Since we now have a total workforce of about 13,000, our executive communications program covers an audience of approximately 1,800 persons ranging from chairman to foreman. We have divided this audience into three categories: general, sales, and plant. The purpose is not to compartmentalize but to tailor the communications and reduce reading time.

We have learned from experience that information of doubtful value to the recipient sets up negative reactions. As an example, information of keen interest to the plant manager probably will not have the same impact on the sales manager—often it will be of no interest at all to him. Consequently, we condense information of marginal value and eliminate that of no value. In competing for people's time, we find it desirable to tailor the communications program for maximum appeal to the various job titles on our distribution list. But in doing this there is no intent to curtail the degree of disclosure to any group.

Companies that do not share basic business information with a large group of employees have their own reasons for this position, and we have no quarrel with them. This, certainly, is a decision the chief executive of each company must reach in light of his own peculiar circumstances. But it is the chief executive, and not someone well down the line, who should make the decision.

In our own case, we have an excellent reason for following our long-standing policy of near-total disclosure. As far back as April 1954, this was noted in our Rockwell Report, a long-established advertising campaign that discusses our company and our attitudes for readers of major financial and news weeklies. At that time we said:

> This policy of sharing information usually closely guarded arises from a conviction that the sound growth of our company depends to a great degree on the team-work of the people who are directly interested in it—

employees, stockholders, jobbers, supply companies, and dealers.

Teamwork, we believe, stems not only from sharing information pertinent to progress toward that goal. You tend to play a better game when you know what the score is.

The only change in our attitude has been that we now believe in this more strongly than ever. Certainly, our own growth would have been much more difficult, if not impossible, had our employees not had a full understanding of our goals and had we not had the cooperation of employees in our various acquisitions, expansions, modernizations, and other forward-looking innovations essential to growth.

This brings us to consideration of the problem of how frequently—or how diligently—to communicate. In our opinion, there can be no hard and fast rules in this area. We have general guidelines for the frequency of our formal communications media, but we can always put out an extra when the information at hand warrants such treatment.

We have a *President's Letter* which is issued at least once a month. This is the channel for communicating directly from the president's office to key operating and staff personnel.

Our vehicle for carrying presidential communications into secondary management levels and into the secondary ranks of plant supervisors is the *Management Letter*, appearing quarterly. The material is essentially the same in both the *Management Letter* and the *President's Letter*, although the depth of the information presented and the emphasis placed on it vary depending on the audience.

Beyond these two publications, each of our divisions has one or more communications vehicles of its own. Typical of these is our Valve Division's *The Direct Line*, a vehicle for the division vice president and product managers in communicating with the sales force.

The distinction we make between our sales communications and our conventional employee communications media is a familiar one. In the former, we strive to provide useful sales pointers for the field force, inform them of significant competitive activity, pass on pertinent market data, and supply other information that pertains directly to the sales job. In employee publications, on the other hand, the goal is to keep employees informed of significant corporate developments, new products, and new factors affecting them as a part of the company and, additionally, to focus on events of significance at the plant level that are of little interest to others in the company.

The president's role of communications chief, of course, extends well beyond the area of employee communications. Whether he likes it or not, the president is, by definition, the spokesman for his company—the last word. His opinions, therefore, should be reflected in all the company's communications.

Generally speaking, we see the president's role as being the same in external communications as it is in internal communications. In communicating to special groups—investors, plant communities, suppliers—as well as to the general public, the president should be just as active a participant as he is in the area of employee communications.

None of this is to suggest that the president should assume full, active, and continuing direction of the communications program. This job is, of course, best left to experts. At Rockwell we feel the best combination is top staff talent augmented by a top public relations agency. Between them, these two groups can effectively counsel the president in establishing policy and take the active role in implementing the communications program on a day-to-day basis.

The important thing is not that the president become enmeshed in the program; the important thing is that he establish the direction and scope of the communications effort, lend his active support where needed, and continually exhort staff personnel to cooperate fully in maintaining constant, effective communications with all key publics.

An especially helpful device, we have found, is the same Rockwell Report mentioned earlier. This started in 1951 as a corporate advertising campaign designed to be a little different and, we hoped, a little more effective than other programs aimed at the business and financial community and at what might be called the upper echelons of the general reading public.

As a result of the Report, we have received approximately 3,000 personal letters over the years—letters that have come from chief executives of more than 300 corporations, from editors and publishers throughout the country, from leading financial and investment counselors, from bankers and investors and potential investors, and from other people who read and apparently are interested in what we have to say. We also receive many requests every year for permission to reprint or quote from the Rockwell Report.

After it had firmly established itself as an effective corporate communications tool, we decided in 1954 to adapt the Report's straightforward format for use at the local level in major plant communities. Now our plant general managers often prepare columns—carrying their photographs and bylines—for use in local newspapers: thus the Statesboro Report for Statesboro, Georgia, or the Hopewell Report for Hopewell, New Jersey. In these columns, the general managers discuss subjects of special interest to local communities. The effect has been to humanize our top local executives and establish the company as one with a real and continuing interest in its employees and in those plant communities where it operates.

Communications is not an easy task. It's one that requires the continuing attention of the president and constant hard work from staff specialists and the public relations agency. Is it all worth the effort? To this we can answer a strong, unqualified "Yes!"

Our experience has been that what is true of internal communications is equally true of external programs. Without exception, the best-known names in American industry are companies that communicate well and continually. They have had effective communications programs for many years and have not lightened their efforts in the face of success.

The value of good communications, then, is firmly established. We believe at Rockwell that presidential effort directed toward improved communications pays dividends in better understanding and more effective relationships with employees and with the key publics outside the company.

"Dear Mr. Galvin":
Businessman Versus College Students

Robert W. Galvin

Dᴇᴀʀ Mʀ. Gᴀʟᴠɪɴ: . . . The young man isn't mad at you; he just doesn't like you. . . ."

These are not the words of a disgruntled Motorola employee or customer. They were written by a college student, not about me in particular, but about businessmen in general. They were written in the course of a series of no-punches-pulled dialogues that I have been carrying on with students from colleges across the country. These dialogues are an effort to build a better climate of understanding between the college man and the businessman; an

Rᴏʙᴇʀᴛ W. Gᴀʟᴠɪɴ is Chairman of the Board and Chief Executive Officer, Motorola Inc. Formerly he was President of the company.

attempt to discover why students frown on business and turn their backs on business careers.

That many college students "don't like us" is not new or startling. This attitude has been analyzed and discussed in magazines and newspapers, on campuses and in corporations. I decided to find out what students are really thinking—and why—after listening to Vernon R. Alden, president of the University of Ohio, forecast a "loss of future leaders" because of negative attitudes about business.

"How can we best offer a thoughtful rebuttal from business?" I asked our vice president of public relations. To explore alternatives, he got together with his people and an outside communications firm. They went out and talked to college students and college administrators on campuses across the country. From these explorations, and from further discussions in my office, evolved the idea of a two-way dialogue in campus newspapers—the medium that offered the best promise of reaching a large audience on its own home ground.

The dialogues began as an open-letter exchange between me and six student correspondents representing their colleges: Harvard, Cornell, Michigan State, University of Southern California, University of Illinois, and University of Texas. The letters—more than 60 that first year— were printed as ads in 29 college papers reaching 300,000 students.

The letter exchange was continued during a second academic year with four correspondents from a new set of schools: Princeton, University of Arizona, Northwestern, and Stanford. In addition, we introduced a series of ten-minute radio dialogues being broadcast over 35 campus stations, with another group of colleges providing the students.

I have had as many face-to-face contacts as possible, too. And these discussions are even more effective. But they're not always practical, and they don't reach nearly as many students.

The opening gambit in the dialogues was a published letter from me. It formally invited the students' participation: "Let's discuss business openly. You express the views of those around you. I'll respond."

Almost to a man, the students challenged the profit motive as selfish. They saw profit as an end rather than as a means to an end. And the students felt they would be bored by business. The corporate world to them was stultifying, offering minimal opportunity for personal growth and little chance to make significant contributions to society. In short, business might be all right for the other fellow, but they had more exciting, more important plans to think about.

As the dialogues progressed, another theme became apparent. Students felt that a person had to wait too long to make his mark in the corporate world. They felt that business wasn't willing to give a man real responsibility. These were truly young men in a hurry, eager to apply and to test the fruits of their education. Their goals weren't primarily monetary. They were action-oriented, and they wanted responsibility and recognition.

They also raised the familiar specter of the organization man. The Cornell University student wrote:

> A college education generally tends to broaden one's outlook, make one more sensitive to the idea of being an individual, and train one to use the mind with as much creativity and imagination as possible.

> Now, what does this newly "humanized" person picture when he views the business world? He sees William H. Whyte, Jr.'s *The Organization Man.* . . . He sees endless interviews and standardized tests where personality traits become more important than intellectual capacities. . . . He sees incessant pressures to conform to the corporate gray-flannel image; pressures that deny him the right of his own individuality. . . .

I reminded the student that Mr. Whyte was concerned about conformity that occurs in *all* large organizations—in government, labor, universities, foundations, and business. "It's a problem that concerns men everywhere," I wrote. "At the moment you're worried about what happens in a corporation. Many of us are worried about what happens to the computer-carded students at our overcrowded colleges and universities."

The exchange of letters brought home a few points to me. I now believe that many students feel threatened and perhaps frightened by the very changes which we think of as challenges. Where we see excitement, they see complexity and confusion. They're frightened by the computer.

They see it as a monster that will rob them of their identity.

This may be particularly true for nontechnical students, the liberal arts or political science majors we are trying to reach. By graduation time, many have already had a taste of impersonality as practiced by the multiversity. They've already seen themselves as one more card in a computer; as being led through depersonalized, television-conducted courses; as bound by "company" rules.

Today's students are highly articulate and extremely well educated. As a result of the media explosion, they have a wide, though often secondhand, view of the world around them. The important thing, however, is that they are concerned about that world and their place in it.

The students are quick to react; eager to learn, to discuss, and to explore. Most of them won't accept pat answers. Some won't accept any answers at all. At this point in their lives they may be seeking personal commitment, but they are also afraid of being taken in—of being sold a bill of goods.

This wariness extends to fields other than business. The prospective teacher knows all about the dictum of "publish or perish." The political science major and prelaw student are aware of government's bureaucracy and the pitfalls in a large law firm. The budding scientist has heard some of the secrets of "grantsmanship." Nevertheless, many students feel that some of these other careers offer more opportunities to function as an individual, more opportunities to get off to a fast start. And many students have greater respect for those who choose one of these careers than for those who choose a business career.

Part of the students' wariness can be attributed to the so-called generation gap. But this phenomenon extends to other segments of our society. The byword is: "Don't trust *anyone* over 30." Generation gaps have, I think, always existed. But today's version is intensified by sweeping technological and social changes.

On the other hand, business faces a credibility and communication gap—at least among certain segments of the campus. It's not that they haven't received the message. They've received too many messages, most of them mass-produced and designed to tell students what they should want instead of asking them what they might like.

It's difficult to measure the results of the dialogues, although my correspondence does indicate that some views are changing as the result of new information, new insights. I've received more than two thousand letters from students, parents, faculty, and businessmen. A few are critical; most are inquisitive. They ask for more information or for a reaction to an opinion or an idea.

These dialogues, which started me thinking along new lines, apparently also started a lot of people thinking—our employees, for example. Copies of the newspaper ads are posted in offices and plants for employee reading. The ads give them a good background on my philosophy and goals. Some employees have told me that the exchange of ideas has prompted them to stop and think, to take a new look at their jobs and their own performance. They now have a better idea of Motorola's place and function in our society. And, more important, they have a clearer idea of their place in the company.

The students' comments have prompted us to take a closer look at some Motorola programs. As a result of complaints about meaningless summer jobs, for example, we have re-evaluated our summer internship program. We want every job to carry real responsibility and to give the young man or woman true experience in corporate life.

We're also looking long and hard at training programs. We're putting ourselves in the new employee's shoes and trying to gauge his reaction to his first year of corporate life. We're trying to provide work opportunities that will encourage creative, independent efforts and reward ability and talent. At the same time, we're pointing up the fact that in many situations there just is no substitute for experience.

Most important to me personally, the program has indicated a need for other businessmen to embark on similar ventures that encourage active and meaningful student participation. These projects should involve first-hand, face-to-face communication. They should provide a forum for an exchange of ideas and opinions.

One objective should be to strike out the gray-flannel stereotype and honestly describe the stresses, the excitement, and the adventure that are part of a business career. The programs should give a more accurate picture of the rewards and personal satisfaction that are an integral part of corporate life.

But, even more important, these programs must communicate business's role and place in our society as a creator of usable wealth, a supplier of human needs, and an employer of people. College students take their personal affluence for granted; they also take the same approach to the nation's affluence. Yet many bright and talented students fail to make the connection between business and this affluence. They fail to see that it's our economic system that provides the bedrock for both material and social progress. They are not aware of the partnership that exists between business and government, both at state and at federal levels.

The young men and women with whom we are trying to communicate will eventually be our nation's leaders. Their respect and understanding are important to business, for they will be influential in determining the rules under which business will be conducted in the decades ahead.

Some members of the dialogue audience will be going into business. We must give them a realistic picture of what to expect. Here, for example, is what I told a senior at the University of Southern California:

> Every corporation knows that in any group hired there will be some who look for security and safety as well as those who look for action and challenge.
>
> It's no secret that companies test the mettle of their new employees to see how well they handle responsibility, deal with people, and make decisions. In business, a man is judged objectively and in relation to other men. This evaluation process is not cold and imper-

sonal, and it's not done by machines. It's based on fact, on performance, on individual ability, on character.

We sell our customers the best possible products we can make. Why not apply the same efforts to introducing young men and women to the business world?

I'm convinced that an employee's first three or four years on the job are crucial ones. I'm appalled by the fact that over 50 percent of college trainees seek new positions during their first two years of work. This is a great waste of time and effort—and some of the blame must be put at the corporate doorstep. Part of the trouble may be that prospects are oversold, that training programs are designed to negate rather than augment the young man's educational experience, that trainees are propagandized and pampered and challenged.

Programs, policies, strategies must be re-evaluated and re-assessed. Moreover, action must then be taken that will affect every level of corporate life. And I'm convinced that the impulse toward this action must originate where policy decisions are made—at the top.

Motorola has many executives who could have conducted the dialogues or visited the students. Any one of them could have done an outstanding job. But the program was my responsibility. As board chairman, I am the one students want to hear, want to evaluate, want to put on the griddle.

There are many different kinds of programs that could effectively "reach" students. The dialogue-by-letter technique is one; another approach is to take the corporation to the campus, or vice versa. A company in the construction industry, for example, could sponsor a series of campus seminars on problems of the cities; seminars where students and faculty could match ideas with the men who are actually restructuring our environment.

Organizations with advanced intracompany education programs could hire college students as training program instructors during the summer months. A student group might also be a highly effective reactor panel for a management training course.

Opportunities for summer employment of college students should be expanded, and the jobs should pay well. They should put students into challenging situations in which they can stand or fall and learn more about themselves in the process.

It's important to bring in students with widely different backgrounds and career choices. The philosophy major may never pursue a career in the automobile industry, but he might spend a productive and educational summer in General Motors' public relations, marketing, or advertising department.

Whenever possible, businessmen—chief executives, especially—should get to the campus. Some executives guest-lecture in graduate and undergraduate schools. More should. Companies located near colleges have, of course, an excellent chance to establish continuing, long-term corporation campus programs.

In addition, efforts should be made to reach faculty

members. Ask them to participate in seminars or to serve as company consultants. Set up summer employment programs for them. A good porportion have never left the campus—they've moved from the back of the classroom to the front. Too often, corporate invitations are extended to the heads of departments. It's time to involve some of the bright young men who are on their way up in the education world.

These are only a few of the things that can be done. The important thing is for more of us to start doing them. We businessmen have always been proud of our problem-solving ability. Here's a fertile field for our talents.

That we are in a youth culture is a fact firmly rooted in the marketing plans of many companies. But we have to sell young people more than our products. We have to sell them goals and ideas and understanding.

One of the most dangerous attitudes expressed by the students is that they take so much of business for granted. They use its products, read its advertisements, have some idea of its productive capacity. But that's about as far as they choose to go.

Some of my colleagues believe that this attitude would quickly change if there were a depression or a serious recession. I'm sure it would. But I'm also sure that there are more positive and constructive ways to get our message across. I don't think we can convince students to care about us until we show that we care about them and want to hear what they have to say.

Students have something to say. Some of their concepts

may be fuzzy; some of their opinions gathered from second-hand sources may be off base. But these ideas and opinions will persist and proliferate until young people see or experience something that generates a change.

It's time to do some gap mending. Our approach should be positive and provocative, honest and forceful. Our job is to make the college student—and every young person—think about business, not only as a career choice, but also as a vital force in society.

The program I have described is now in its third year. I have been joined by Russell De Young, chairman of Goodyear Tire & Rubber Company, and H. D. Doan, president of Dow Chemical Company. Our association provides additional business viewpoints and allows for expansion of the program to reach more students.

Getting Started in Politics:
A President's Guide

John W. Rollins

In 1960, I ran for governor of Delaware. Since then, many friends have asked me if being involved in politics damaged my personal or business reputation. As far as I can determine, politics hasn't hurt me at all—even though I lost the election.

I assume that the sincere concern for my reputation is rooted in the traditional feeling among businessmen that the typical politician is a man who couldn't hold a job in industry. But the arrival on the political scene of men such

JOHN W. ROLLINS is President and Chairman, Rollins Leasing Corp., Wilmington, Delaware. He has been Lieutenant Governor of the State of Delaware.

as Michigan's George Romney, Governor Russell W. Peterson of Delaware, and Senator Stuart Symington of Missouri has done much to change this notion.

If there is something missing in our politics (and the businessman's description of the politician says there is), it is not so much the fault of those who are in politics as it is the fault of those who are not.

There is a temptation to point to Romney and others like him and to conclude that business leaders are indeed active in politics. What is missing, the reasoning goes, cannot be blamed on them. This, of course, is not entirely true. Business leaders, particularly presidents and members of top management, generally shy away from politics. As a result, politics too often has become the plaything of those who have the least to contribute.

Look at any effective corporate president and you will find many of the same talents characteristic of our finest political leaders. He has the education, the prestige, the practical experience, and, perhaps most important, the ability to work with and through other people. He is, therefore, the ideal man to roll up his sleeves and get into politics—even if he has to start at the precinct level.

As a beginner, he must enter politics with an air of humility and a desire to learn and to work. Because he has reached the top in his corporate career, he may be tempted to believe that he should be able to transfer his credentials and prerogatives automatically. Unfortunately, success in business does not assure success—or even competency—in the political world. Nothing is more harmful in politics than an obvious and aggressive takeover attitude. Instead, the political beginner should expect to put in an apprenticeship before he can hope to become a skilled politician or even to understand the mechanisms and principles of politics.

This is a bitter pill for many executives. At every political level, however, there are challenges to stir a top executive's creativity and fulfill his desire for accomplishment.

Although he may be serving his apprenticeship in a secondary post, he should not be shy about expressing his ideas. When it comes to forming a platform or selecting candidates, an executive is likely to carry a good deal of weight because of his ability to define the issues and to present them clearly. His natural gifts as a leader will not be wasted or go unnoticed.

The newcomer should not feel unappreciated, however, if his suggestions are sometimes pigeonholed. Politics is a rough-and-tumble affair. Ideas compete with each other, not only in terms of logic, but also in terms of compromise —the catalyst of government.

Unfortunately, the word "compromise" has lost a good deal of its original meaning. Some regard it as a synonym for "cowardice." This is a dangerous assumption. Politics has been described as the art of the possible. Every successful politician has learned that he must get his job done by winning and holding the respect and confidence of his associates. To complicate his job further, his associates usually are volunteers who rank as equals when decisions are being made. The newcomer should learn to think to himself: "Here is the ideal, what I would like; but this is what I am likely to get."

He probably will be startled in his early days in politics to discover how many prejudices he has. In his business career, a president solves many problems by drawing on the lessons he learned and the techniques he discovered in past problem-solving situations. In politics, however, he will find himself in a virtually new field. He must learn that often his way is not the only way. Whether the job is the framing of a campaign platform or the nomination of a candidate, an open mind and the ability to adjust to less than perfect solutions are important attributes for success.

Some political scientists, particularly those from abroad, charge that the American two-party system prohibits the selection of the best candidates. They say it produces candidates who are least likely to offend important segments of their parties. This charge is both true and false.

Frequently, a leading candidate for a nomination antagonizes one or more groups within his organization and thereby threatens to splinter it. Perhaps the veteran politicians don't like the bright young candidate championed by the business executive—the newcomer. The politicians may be right. Perhaps the businessman likes the candidate simply because he has the same opinions or a similar background. Out of the conflict emerges a compromise candidate. He may not be as good as the businessman's original choice. On the other hand, he may be better.

The newcomer should not be overly disappointed when

his candidate is not selected. The chances are that his party's choice probably is a much better one because he participated in the selection. Ideally, the candidate should represent all factions within the party. Since getting elected is a matter of life and death in the political arena, a compromise candidate can run an effective campaign only if all the factions within the party unite behind his personal banner.

In every political contest there are significant segments of a party which, at first, fail to rally behind the nominated candidate. In the 1960 Presidential election, some liberals in the Democratic party didn't rally behind President Kennedy until it was almost too late. In the two previous elections, many conservatives in the Republican party gave less than full support to General Eisenhower. But General Eisenhower was able to win because of his strong support by the dominant middle-of-the-road segment of the party. In 1968 Senator Eugene McCarthy's supporters found it difficult to accept Vice President Hubert Humphrey as a candidate. This contributed heavily to Humphrey's defeat. In the case of Kennedy and Eisenhower, the respective parties were able to close ranks. All the party leaders did not agree with the choices, but they recognized—in sufficient time—that their candidates were the best possible selections and that the important job now was to get them elected.

Although no two campaigns are ever exactly alike, every campaign (whether it's successful or not) depends on the ability of the party to collect campaign funds. By virtue of his so-called social connections, a president often is asked to help raise campaign funds. Here are a few rules for successful fund raising.

The first hurdle to get over is the self-conscious notion that when you ask for money you are asking for yourself personally. If you can subordinate this self-conscious aspect of fund raising, half the problem is solved. Simply remember that you are really asking a person to contribute to a cause that is important to him as well as to you.

It is essential, of course, for the fund raiser to have donated money himself. It is difficult to look a man in the eye and ask for money when you haven't contributed yourself.

Candidates often are handicapped by lack of money to carry out their campaigns effectively. Too often, a candidate can't run (no matter how qualified he is) simply because he can't raise money. Raising funds to help a worthwhile candidate present his views to the public is an important job. And it's a perfect job for a corporate president.

At some time in the future, you may be called upon to be your party's candidate for an elective office. This is an exciting and rewarding experience, win or lose. Even defeat does not sour all the time and effort you will lavish on the campaign.

Running for local political office is an excellent way for a businessman to get started on a side career in politics.

The possibilities include such posts as those of mayor, councilman, county supervisor, state representative, or state senator.

Many businessmen are attracted to a position on the local school board. School-board campaigns, however, are often the most competitive and hardest fought, and it is not difficult to understand why. For one thing, school boards often spend the bulk of the municipal budget. For another, few things are more important to most people than the education of their children. When tempers flare during a school-board election, the repercussions can linger for years.

Many businessmen ask if running for political office is likely to jeopardize their personal popularity. Obviously, no political decision can be popular with everyone. The person who is concerned with being popular at all times has no place in the political arena. But an executive who reaches top management probably has already accepted the fact that his personal popularity in his own company certainly must be less than overwhelming if he does his job.

The man in politics must realize that both his official and his personal acts are subject to the glaring scrutiny of the press, radio, and television. A family man going into politics had better help his family grow some thick skin. His only real security will be the recognition that he is seeking public office to do a job that needs to be done.

In addition to helping select a candidate, participating in a campaign, or running for office, an executive can work for specific political causes. Many businessmen have become active in politics through their interest in school bonds. Other favorite causes include better parks, modern zoning laws, better methods of taxation—even international issues involving war and peace.

The businessman who supports a cause often finds that he is championing an unpopular one. But important areas of social progress have often resulted from so-called unpopular causes. They include movements for child-labor laws, the vote for women, and many others. Every businessman must search his own conscience to determine whether an issue deserves his personal support, regardless of its immediate popularity.

One of the finest features of our political system is that membership in our parties is not based on ancestral, economic, geographic, or even historic lines. Neither party can claim complete and exclusive loyalty to any specific ideological or economic objective. There are nearly as many wealthy Americans who support the Democratic party as support the Republican party. Even organized labor has supported some Republican candidates. This was the case in the successful 1968 campaign of Richard Nixon.

The Democratic and Republican parties are reasonable cross sections of our society. In neither party do all members think alike. In fact, the liberal wings of both parties have more in common with each other than with the opposite wings within their own parties.

To many businessmen, this is reason enough to remain on the sidelines, free to pick and choose the best of both parties from a vantage point safely above the political arena. The advocate of nonpartisanship (call him the independent) is really disdainful of our two-party system. He supports what he considers the best candidates of both parties.

By its very nature, however, politics is competitive and partisan. It is a race between two groups to win a public mandate to carry out a program. Candidates do not exist in an organizational vacuum. They exist by virtue of their selection and support by their party. Supporting the candidate without supporting his party hurts the candidate because it deprives him of strong, united backing. And this often is the difference between defeat and success.

The independent or nonpartisan advocate is capable of reacting to both good and bad decisions of either party. But he is unable to take that important extra step—to take part in the making of these decisions. To do this, a businessman —or any citizen—must work within his party to elect the best possible candidates.

Father Was a Genius, but ...

Edward A. Ring

It took me several years, after my father died, to sort out my thoughts about him and appraise him for what he was. A genius. An indefatigable producer. A proud and dedicated man. And a very bad manager—judged by modern theories.

His campaign to take over the Circle F Manufacturing Company, founded in 1904 to make electrical wiring devices, was typical of the single-minded way he went after his goals. It took him 15 years—from 1937 to 1952—to buy out his original group of investors. He increased Circle F's assets from $400,000 to $9 million during the 27 years that he either owned or controlled the company. But in his last

Edward A. Ring is President and Chairman of the Board, Circle F Industries, Trenton, New Jersey.

years he lacked daring. He would rather sit on his money than risk it on growth.

Looking back, I see my father as a benevolent despot, which was the style of his time. I admired the brilliance with which he directed production while bemoaning the problems he provoked by holding the reins too tightly. I often wondered if *my* way would ever be given a chance.

I was the marketing director and the only other stockholder, but my position gave me little authority and lots of frustration. I quit three times in disgust. Each time my father would get me back, usually by promising to build another plant so we could increase production and put some of our marketing plans into effect. But the plants were always half as large as they should have been. Soon I gave up even wanting to try out my management theories.

My first long-term defection—during which I ran my own company—ended when my father offered to buy me out in an exchange of stock. He seemed to be mellowing; so I accepted. That was in 1952. I soon realized that he was too devoted to his authoritarian habits to really change. I had to wait to try out my new ideas.

My initial weeks in the presidency consisted mainly of holding the pieces together. I studied the organization, talked to managers, toured the plants, and examined the books. I invited the top executives to my home for dinner and asked them what I could do to help them run their departments better. The answer in every case: "Let me run my own department and take up only important matters with you." I also learned that our spectacular growth had camouflaged some deep flaws.

For one thing, we were too big for one-man management. My father knew this, but he wouldn't ask for help. And he played one man off against the other. He would walk through a plant and ask an employee why he was doing a job in a certain way. This would upset the craftsman, undercut the foreman, and breed distrust.

The flaw that could have proved fatal in the long run, though, lay in my father's orientation to the present. Our product line was unnecessarily restricted and our older plants badly cramped. But the machinery was efficient and we were one of the most profitable companies in the industry. Trouble was, we were borrowing from the future and living off the past. There was no management structure, no management depth, no plans for the future.

In January 1965, two months after my father's death, I took our key men to Atlantic City, New Jersey, for three days to ask ourselves questions. The meeting was preceded by several weeks of research: studying our competitors' positions; getting a fix on where we stood in relation to them; identifying the innovators in the many product lines that make up our business (we alone make over 15,000 different electrical devices).

The meeting was a classic company self-analysis: What are our strengths and weaknesses? Where are we going? How will we get there and how long will it take? We came up with some answers—and even more questions.

What's more, the men at the meeting—men who for 25 years had been responsible for profits, production, growth —*for the first time* received information about the company's financial condition. My father had given neither information nor authority nor titles. Only one of the nine men was an officer, yet each held a key position. Now I filled them in on the entire financial picture for the past 15 years. I told them how we stood against our competitors. I briefed them on sales and earnings on a department-by-department basis.

We came out of the meeting with agreement on these eight corporate objectives:

- To make *Fortune*'s list of top 500 companies by 1980, if not sooner.
- To earn at least 20 percent on net investment.
- To earn at least 10 percent on sales after taxes.
- To expand our product line.
- To build a new public image. (Although we were the largest taxpayer in Trenton, New Jersey, we were not really well known in the community.)
- To make ourselves better known in the industry and impress contractors and architects (our industry customers) with the fact that we will make what they want, not just sell them what we make.
- To improve our relations with the unions.
- To develop better managers.

From the Atlantic City session came the idea for weekly operations committee meetings to serve as a basic top management communications channel. At these meetings I would ask everyone around the table to tell what was going on in his division and to describe his problems. Each man gradually began to get a feel for the other man's job.

I remember feeling rather pleased with my progress until an incident made me realize that the old distrust planted by my father's authoritarian habits was still there. On this occasion somebody said cynically, "The only purpose of these meetings is to bring you up to date on what's going on." Disappointed, but realizing that sermonizing wasn't going to help, I simply replied, "If that's what you think, fine. In the meantime, let's keep on telling each other what we're doing. This will fulfill the principal function of the meetings—to exchange information."

I should have known it would take a while to develop the cooperation I was looking for. What can you expect when you think of what they had been used to?

My father loved working out every detail. So it was natural for him to manage through a command: "Do it this way." Later, if something went wrong, he'd call in the person he thought responsible and ask why. "The factory didn't produce what we asked for," was the man's answer. My father would then call in the factory manager and report the complaint to him. The factory manager's answer: "Well, those other guys didn't do such-and-such." By the time my father got through, *he* knew what was going on, but he had everybody doubting everybody else in the process. I'm sure it wasn't intentional. His purpose was to get information, but the result was a tremendous amount of static.

Historically, many companies with driving chief executives have been predominantly production-oriented. My father's certainly was. "All you have to do is build a better product and people will buy it," he'd say. "Any moron can sell." This may have been true at a more primitive level of industrial society, but a company today must be market-oriented to succeed.

The real shift to modern marketing techniques had to await my succession to the presidency. Our goal was to create market demand, not merely to respond to it. In our business this requires a strong engineering department. In two years we increased the engineering section from 3 people to 45.

We're learning from our customers. From time to time we have invited architects, engineers, contractors—people who buy our products—to meet with our engineering, sales, and production people. These sessions help us determine what kind of products the customer needs and wants. And we're learning from consultants, too. My father wouldn't use them. It didn't occur to him that if he didn't know the answer he could find it somewhere.

Our new management approach stresses delegation of authority. This requires a structured organization—something that we never really had before. I've reorganized the company along functional lines, starting at the top and working down through divisions and departments. And we are still reorganizing, still making changes.

A key move was the appointment of a four-man executive group composed of my new assistant, now vice president of engineering; a financial adviser, now vice president of finance; the secretary-treasurer; and the manager of manufacturing, who became the vice president of manufacturing. "If I'm not here, this group will have to run the company," I announced. Then, as though to drive home the urgency of the problem of delegation and succession, I was struck down by a heart attack just seven months after taking over. For 15 weeks the company ran without me. No one told me what was going on at Circle F, and I didn't ask.

We're now giving special attention to management development. For almost every top management job there's a man ready to step in, and we're building management depth by extending the manpower inventory and appraisal system down through the lower echelons of the organization. I don't hesitate to bring in outside people, but I prefer to promote from within for obvious reasons: It uses the valuable assets of experience and boosts morale. To do this requires (1) identifying and testing capabilities, (2) setting standards, and (3) holding out incentives.

One of the most effective ways to test a man's abilities is to assign him a task outside his area. I've taken an engineering man and asked him to tackle a personnel problem, and I've asked a personnel man to investigate a manufacturing problem. I've even taken someone in manufacturing and asked him to solve a sales problem. Although these are special assignments, they are not created artificially. Besides helping me measure the individuals involved, they provide broadening experience.

With the emphasis on delegation come standards of performance. Every division has its own goals, and every manager is responsible for his group's performance. This is an important first step in implementing the profit-center concept that is now guiding us with a sound data processing system; every manager has the rapid information feedback he needs to make the profit-center plan work. And our incentive program based on profitability means that every manager has a stake in the success of his operation.

Our company has never been more vigorous than it is today, but in recent years we have not been keeping pace with the growth rate in our industry. We are trying to catch up, but profits do not always increase in proportion to sales. This is not surprising. We have been investing in people, sophisticated equipment, new plants.

The productivity rate of our six plants in Trenton is among the highest in the industry. This is good for profits, of course, but I don't like what it suggests—crowded conditions for employees. Can you imagine not even having the space to put in a soda machine? Yet this inability to satisfy readily understandable employee demands, I believe, is one of the reasons that helped bring on the costly seven-week strike—our first since we were organized in 1940—that we had in early 1967.

We have since been learning how to motivate people and how to satisfy more than just their basic animal needs. We've made a start with a pension plan, participation in employee recreation activities, and programs to boost employee morale.

Our new plants in Pageland, South Carolina, and Bordentown, New Jersey, have helped the overcrowding in Trenton; but, along with our recent acquisitions, they also are straining our still-new organization. No sooner are areas of responsibility defined than they have to be redefined. People just getting used to one hierarchy have to adjust to new ones. These problems are making us realize the importance of communications, preferably the face-to-face variety. The weekly operations committee meetings that preceded my heart attack have been resumed on a monthly basis. I also meet monthly with division heads and their key people.

From time to time we expand the committee to 35 or 40 people. This enlarged group is strictly an open forum to exchange information on major problems. Also, to further broaden the communications base, we hold dinner meetings with the entire management staff from assistant foremen up. I speak to them about Circle F Industries, as the company is now called, and an outside speaker talks on some business topic.

To become better known in the community—and to attract good people—we are using institutional advertising, FM music programs, a direct mail campaign to local thought leaders, and a speakers' bureau. In addition, we even sponsored a spectacular art show in the State Museum in Trenton. There are subtle but significant signs that the communications program is paying off. Employees seem prouder than ever to work for us, and it shows up in reduced turnover and absenteeism.

When I became president, 39 people reported to me, and I made all the decisions. I worked seven days a week, and I didn't count how many hours a day. I tried to work my reforms into a few months—and my heart went on strike.

Now, only eight executives report to me and I am much closer to my goal: to make Circle F a streamlined growth company. But I'm afraid that, like my father, I won't stop meddling as long as I'm here.

One Man Show ...
with a Cast of Thousands

Charles E. Zimmerman

It happened during a convention in Puerto Rico, at a cocktail party in a friend's home. When a sudden pain shot through my stomach, I at first attributed it to those frozen daiquiris, but when the pain hit my chest and arms, I collapsed. My host stretched me out on a couch in the living room and called a doctor. Next morning I awoke in a hospital oxygen tent. I had had a classic coronary, that specter haunting many chief executives.

When the president of a giant corporation suffers a

Charles E. Zimmerman is Chairman and President, Consultants & Designers Inc., New York City, since November 1968 a subsidiary of the Greyhound Corporation.

heart attack, he has plenty of backstops to carry on for him. But what's the impact on a company like mine that was founded as a one-man business and long run with one-man leadership? That's what I worried about in a Puerto Rican hospital for five weeks. I was kept at home, also, for two months, and as I lay in bed I wondered if my company would fall apart without me.

I was 33 years old when I formed the company in 1950 and went into the technical services business. All I had was a secretary to help me when I set for myself the goal of getting enough business to keep 50 designers and draftsmen working. I had barely become established when the Korean War broke out, and I was hard pressed to keep up with the demand for technical brainpower. But within six months I had reached my goal and promptly set a new one for the company at 100 men. In 1960, after I had far exceeded this objective too, we went into the temporary office help field, a natural extension of our service-oriented company. A year later, we expanded into the exhibit designing and manufacturing business through an acquisition.

As we approached $7 million a year in sales, I appointed a general manager, division heads, and a financial man to supervise internal auditing. Profits that weren't plowed back as working capital were invested in people. Yet the company was an extension of one man—Charles Zimmerman. Brainpower clients, particularly, wanted to deal with The Boss. My position was like that of a chief surgeon who guides many skilled hands and who personally directs every part of the operation, from preoperative consultations to the last stitches.

But there are limitations to what any one man can do; so I appointed an executive vice president. And, to dispel any doubts as to the importance I attached to the post, I made it clear that he would someday take over as my successor—if he measured up. Meantime, I held firmly onto the policy and administrative reins. For I enjoyed my job too much, and had too much confidence in my own ability to operate the business, to give up my roles as policy maker, image maker, chief planner, operations boss, and financial head. So in 1961, when net sales reached $9 million, Charles Zimmerman—producer, director, and star of the show—collapsed under the load.

Recuperating at home after my coronary, I read reports from my office and was glad to learn that things were going well. Or was I? A lurking suspicion that sooner or later somebody would foul things up and everybody would be out of a job soon gave way to touches of jealous frustration. As I studied the encouraging progress reports, I began to wonder how indispensable I really was. But I didn't allow myself the luxury of idle self-pity for too long. Before my attack, I was considering going public to get the capital the company needed to keep pace with growing demand. Now I used my recuperation period to negotiate with the under-writers.

It was the thought of going public as much as anything else that forced me to admit, even before my attack, that Consultants & Designers Inc. could no longer be a solo show. Investors buy more than a company's earning power. They also have a stake in the management that's going to keep the company going and growing. I knew that, with stockholders as my partners, I had to be more concerned with building up my top management staff and delegating more responsibilities to managers at all levels.

So I looked for men with experience. But, like any business that is blazing fresh trails, we were in a field so new that trained specialists were virtually unavailable. I hired raw talent instead and refined it with on-the-job training in the ranks. I gave each budding executive just enough time to absorb one job before moving him along to another. Tender loving care and sharp criticism were dispensed according to the needs of the moment. The sweetener was always a salary fully commensurate with the job.

The proof that I had a workable formula for developing good managers was little personal consolation for my company's continued smooth performance without me. Nevertheless, heeding my doctor's warnings, I let go more and more control when I returned. I gave up overseeing day-to-day operations, leaving this chiefly to our executive vice president and others on the corporate staff. I stopped supervising the daily cash flow, as well as day-to-day new business. New clients did not know me personally, and I stayed out of the picture. No longer did I pound the table and insist on having everything brought to me. Nor did I deal directly with lower-echelon employees' problems. After I'd recovered from the shock of discovering that I was replaceable, I was glad to leave such chores to others. I was no longer the man who pushed *all* the buttons.

Of course, I retained what I considered really essential functions. To perhaps 25 of our major clients I am still the top man, and they want to talk to me on occasion. I also keep close watch on the presidents of our three subsidiaries, our five division managers, and our corporate officers—all of whom work under our executive vice president. But only the treasurer, the executive vice president, and my assistant report directly to me.

While shedding former responsibilities, I've taken on new roles, especially in relations between our company and our stockholders, bankers, accountants, and lawyers. I concentrate on the continuing development of the corporate management team. I also have more time for our acquisition program, and in the past four years we have absorbed six other companies.

As we continue to grow, I have to admit that some aspects of the job are over my head. I'm not an expert on taxes and pensions, on direct mail and labor laws. Skilled specialists must be utilized in these fields. Some authority must be entrusted to carefully chosen people as insurance against accidents like mine. Any company head who works 16 hours a day trying to push all the buttons is destined for tranquilizers, alcoholism, or premature retirement. He can't possibly stay sharp on his job that long.

This kind of insurance entails a high premium, both financial and intellectual, but it paid off in the case of my illness. I know that the drastic change in my role has made me both a different and a better company president. With the day-to-day routine off my back, I can focus on important areas such as long-range planning and company image. After an acquisition, I can concentrate on steering the new subsidiary into its proper niche within the organization. With the luxury of time, I have the opportunity to mull over major decisions rather than make them intuitively as I often used to do. I have more time to explore the thinking of experts.

Not long ago, we were trying to acquire another company, but I couldn't arrive at the right price formula. An investment adviser gave me the answer during a lively lunch. But it takes time to explore ideas with knowledgeable people. You can't do that unless you strip yourself of nonessentials.

In my present role, I have attained a broader perspective. I've begun, for example, to appreciate what our competitors are doing. In the past, I had time to hate them but not to understand them. I can be more critical, too. When you assume all the responsibilities and make all the big decisions, it's hard to be objective. If your decisions are bad, you rationalize; if they're good, you pat yourself on the back. But, when you delegate a function, you can be a legitimate critic.

In my new role, I still see the same amount of paper on my desk. The difference is that the paper I now see is more important. I have more time to decide just what I want to know, and I am asking better questions. So are our other executives. We've developed a management team that's out shooting elephants, not rabbits. We're a mature organization now, no longer a brash upstart. I don't believe any of us realized this till recently, when we had our first retirement.

Having shed so many office stints, I do more traveling,

once a luxury for me. At least two-fifths of my time is now spent in the field—visiting our offices throughout the United States and Canada, as well as the offices of our major customers. My travels set an example for our salesmen. Getting around, not sitting in a cozy office, gets business done.

A president who gives up too much authority often creates more operating problems than he bargained for. Passing along responsibilities merely because it is "the thing to do" is risky, not only for the president, but for the company. Our organization, I discovered, is no different. Once some leases negotiated by one of our division managers turned out to be costly mistakes. Another time, an overeager-beaver salesman incorrectly specified the capabilities of some of our technicians for a project—another expensive mistake. Such incidents probably would not occur if I were doing everything myself, but that's the gamble every president must take.

I've learned, however, that delegating responsibility does not mean giving up control. Whenever I give authority to a man, I keep a string on him. I let the string out slowly, longer and longer, never letting go until I feel reasonably sure that the man's judgment is reliable. I still review all major contracts, and I sometimes find it hard to keep from rushing in to help clinch a deal. When I see something done incorrectly, I try to evaluate the damage. Am I being overcritical? Can the error be justified? I talk it over with the manager in charge, but I don't take over the responsibility for the job.

I now take several vacations a year, but I still put in ten

hours a day on my job, trimmed down as it is. I still like to think that there isn't a job in the place that I can't do better than the man handling it. I would like to be a one-man show, but I have to admit that one man can do only so much. So I force myself to walk away. I love my work too much to give up any responsibility easily.

Looking back, I believe my coronary came at a propitious time. Our company had expanded enough that I was ready to streamline my job. The illness only hastened a natural evolution toward the development of a strong management team headed by a stronger, more professional chief executive.

I Grow with My Job

Elmer L. Winter

Every chief executive has his own ideas on how to get things done—and done well. But, as business grows more and more complex, we are all faced with the same problem: how to find the time to keep up with the growing demands of the job. From experience, I have developed my own techniques for growing with the job before it outgrows me.

I found out early that a moderate, steady pressure spread over a longer time span each day generates better results, with less wear and tear on myself and everyone else concerned, than does alternating between high-pressure activity and get-away-from-it-all relaxation. You might say I operate on DC. You don't have to undergo an emotional

Elmer L. Winter is President, Manpower, Milwaukee, Wisconsin.

lobotomy to adopt a direct-current approach. All you have to do is adopt the kind of emotional posture that lets you get things done.

Up to the time I co-founded Manpower in 1948, I followed the more common method of executive operation: work at top pressure for hours at a stretch, then relax completely away from the office—at a club or at home. But I sensed gradually that this did not suit either my personality or the requirements of my job. As these requirements grew, I knew that I must find a way to relieve the mounting emotional pressure and at the same time increase my personal efficiency. So I relieved the pressure by stretching out my workday from 9 hours to 12. This replaced the agonized, forced flow of activity with a more natural, even flow of drive and creativity that helps me do my job with greater certainty.

Experience also has taught me to put important things first. Too many chief executives file away their most important problems in the back of their minds, to be taken up again when they have time, while keeping the front of their minds open to new, often less important matters that come up. This is the reverse of what I consider the most effective executive manner. I wade into the most difficult problems first. This prevents executive pile-up and last-minute fire fighting.

There was a time, though, when I thought it wise to get the little things out of the way first. I learned the hard way that this destroys efficiency. About five weeks before an annual meeting a few years ago, I sat at my desk going through a stack of old papers, pulling out memos on ten minor, unfinished projects. Then and there I vowed to get these out of the way. I failed, however, to set a deadline for myself, and two days later was still wrestling with the last few. I had lost nearly three entire working days trying to clean up ten minor projects while the annual meeting drew closer.

The seriousness of the situation did not dawn on me until later, when I found that in addition to neglecting the planning for my personal role at the meeting I had neglected to follow up on several executives who were handling some important projects related to the meeting. The importance of tackling first things first became apparent at that moment. Now, when I have important things to do, I keep them in the forefront of my mind so that they brush aside less important matters as I move along.

Acquiring this habit took real effort, for it is human nature—and the core of the learning process—to work from the easy to the difficult. But managing calls for exactly the opposite approach. Managing is the application of knowledge, not the acquiring of it. I was spending my time picking up leaves instead of plowing the ground.

The principle of putting important things first applies as well to personal matters. It means leading a life organized around objectives and interweaving the personal with the business. I find that if I am so organized, my family and its demands pose no insoluble problems. In fact, members of my family reorganize their lives to mesh with mine.

An executive's working rhythm can be unhinged by a

sharp change of pace when he reaches home. The change shatters the working rhythm—and hence momentum—built up during the day. This rhythm is as important to the chief executive as it is to workers in the plant. The idea that work should be kept totally separate from personal life seems to be getting increasingly prevalent, but work is part of the fun of living and there is nothing wrong with discussing work at lunch, at the dinner table, at a party, or with weekend guests. Sometimes, I admit, business talk jolts some guests or associates, but they get used to it and simply return the favor. It actually relaxes them—as it does me—to feel the thread of usefulness running through our lives.

My first-things-first principle is put into practice first thing every morning. Getting up at 6 A.M., I take a pad and pencil and outline a problem that must be solved, working out solutions (some of them, admittedly, farfetched). This gives me a better view of the problem and some helpful hints on picking the right solution. I approach each problem as I would the opening of virgin territory in a new country, never presuming to know the best way to go without first scouting ahead to see where each route leads.

Parking ten blocks from the office and walking the rest of the way gives me time to reflect—and it helps keep my weight down, too. The first hour in the office—8 to 9 A.M.—is reserved to organize my day and to get the most pressing matters out of the way. "No phone calls or other interruptions except for emergencies" is the general rule. The remainder of the day follows the task-oriented concept: Work toward accomplishing meaningful objectives, moving quickly to tackle the more difficult problems first. My secretary and subordinates are trained to prework as much of a problem as they can so that I am merely presented with alternatives awaiting my decision.

The rule is: Bring me no problems until they have been studied to the point of decision. This has two advantages: (1) It conserves my time; and (2) it gets subordinates deeply involved in the heavier aspects of management, thereby preparing them to take my place and make decisions during my long and frequent trips on the road. This minimizes the cult of personality—the dependence of an organization on a single person—that plagues companies as well as governments.

It sounds paradoxical, but I rest on the run. This requires a conscious effort on my part to reject tension as a motivating force, to keep cool and calm despite disappointments and frustrations, and to apply pressure on subordinates without getting emotional. All easier said than done, to be sure. I urge my subordinates to set goals that lie just beyond their reach. This is motivation by stretching, and they invariably rise to the challenge. To those on the receiving end, this may sound like chronic complaining and ingratitude for work well done. But, in most cases, people are eventually grateful.

Timetables and time-bound schedules can do more to produce ulcers than any single factor in an executive's life. This is especially true if we fight time or fight to pack more time into a given hour. I work out a timetable based on completion of tasks by a certain time, to which the daily schedule—being here at ten and there at noon—is subordi-nated. This helps me to keep a mental picture of *tasks* ahead, not appointments.

Sometimes I have to stretch my timetable out of shape a little to accommodate the unexpected problem. This means rescheduling or even canceling appointments. Some of the appointments, as it often turns out, prove not to have been so necessary after all.

I once had to choose between keeping an appointment with an important prospective customer (made at his re-quest) or working on an important talk before an invest-ment analyst group. The event was a week away, and work on the talk could have been postponed. There were other objectives, however, that loomed between then and my talk before the analysts. If I set aside the talk, I would lose my train of thought and interrupt my timetable. The problem: Which activity was more important? The answer: The prospective customer. But the timing was wrong. I asked if he would agree to change our appointment. It turned out that he had the same problem I did, and he welcomed the opportunity to change the date. I used the extra time to find out a little more about what he had in mind, and I was better prepared for our appointment.

Using time to full advantage means making use of every opportunity: dashing off some memos instead of reading a magazine while on an airplane, using Saturday mornings for quiet reflection and planning, or brainstorming a prob-lem as I drive to the office.

I avoid conferences as much as possible because they

tend to be great time wasters. Why? Because there are usually more than enough people at any conference to make the decisions. Somebody is always afraid to "leave out Jack. His feelings might be hurt:" So Jack is brought in, although his interest may be peripheral. There is also too much hidden agenda in the form of personal problems (self-assertion, defense mechanisms) beneath the surface at most conferences. When I must attend a meeting, I move in and out, staying just long enough to spark it, challenge an assumption, and keep it moving toward decision. This in-and-out method is my own way of coping with the time demands of conferences. It is an effective compromise between avoiding them completely or participating fully in them. The presence of the president gives the meeting a sense of urgency, while his absence enables hidden agenda to work themselves out under less tension.

The problem of conserving executive time also involves community activities. At one time, I kept a sharp line between community and business life. But this was very frustrating, because the abrupt switch from one to the other made it difficult to evaluate when I had had enough of one or the other. I spent a considerable amount of energy in deciding when to begin one and drop the other. In addition, I was pulled in different directions at the same time by the divergent demands of business and community. I later realized that whatever work I performed for agencies outside the business should be limited primarily to what I could do in and from my office.

Community activities, if handled the wrong way, can

play hob with an executive's need to conserve time and energy. After an exhausting three-hour dinner-and-report meeting of a community agency, I realized how little that meeting had required my presence. It was a classic example of out-of-office work handled in typical conference style involving numerous individuals, each with his ax to grind. Now I restrict myself to committee posts where the real work can be done by phone from the office through sub-committees, luncheon meetings, and written reports. Less public exposure, perhaps, but greater satisfaction from getting more things done in less time. Also, I try to limit my participation in community activities to where I have some special knowledge that will bring expertise to the activity.

You might think that spreading out into community service would impede an executive's forward momentum. The reverse is true. It is like spreading your sails to catch more wind. A business is conducted, not in a vacuum, but amidst the storm and stress brought on by social change. Being involved in the community helps me to understand the complex trends in our society. In fact, I constantly find that I gain more through enhanced understanding of my business than I put into a volunteer project in the form of work or ideas. Creativity is stimulated, and in a service enterprise such as ours, creative ideas are everything.

Taking time for personal relationships also helps increase my feel for the wants of others—and hence my accuracy in deciding whether the public wants this or that type of service, whether the firm should diversify in some new area, or whether we should go along with new public relations or advertising ideas.

There also have been unexpected dividends from a hobby that I took up back in the early days of the business. I remember complaining to my wife at the time that I felt like a human data processing machine. "Why not take up art?" she said. "Join a businessmen's art class and see what you can do." Nothing could have been further from my mind. "I can't even draw a straight line," I protested. "Besides, I have no interest in art." But I followed her advice, and after a year of classwork I discovered a new way to creativity through painting, sculpture, and mosaics. I formerly believed that there is no apparent connection between art and business life. But, as a result of my deep interest in art, my business thinking has been greatly enriched. Creativity in one area of a person's life seems to spill over in other areas. This explains why art stimulates ideas I can use in my job as president.

True creativity, I discovered, must be spontaneous and self-motivated. As chief executive, let your people know that you welcome creativity. But don't try to force it. Be sure that your people work in an atmosphere where creativity can flourish. Don't say to yourself or let others say to you, "I don't have time to be creative." Time does not fetter the creative spirit.

The real problem all presidents have in common is not one of availability of time. It's how to make the most creative use of every moment of available time. Find the personal communion spot that stimulates your own creativity and the free flow of ideas. (The mountains challenge me and free my imagination.) The key to creativity, in personal as well as company life, is not to seek a comfortable mode of operation but to reach constantly beyond your grasp in the hot pursuit of excellence.

Index